Texcot

Dreams, Lies and Fraud

Richard Velasquez

Dedication

To my family

Thank you for your love and support for over 25 years of Bureau life. The stress and pressure of law enforcement was probably tougher on you than me.

———————————————

To the Dallas Division support personnel and street agents

In 2002, the spring just after 9-11, I was invited to a first responder "Hero Day" at an elementary school in Plano, Texas. A first-grade boy asked me if I was a hero. I responded, "No, but I work on a squad with heroes." Continue to fight the good fight, finish the race, keep the faith… 1 Timothy 4:7

Table of Contents

Author's Note

The information contained in this book has been drawn from my own personal experiences, witness interviews and the review of official documents, including court records and other public information sources. For security purposes, some dates, locations, times and names have been changed where appropriate.

Any reference to law enforcement tactics is considered common knowledge and is viewed as known acts published in the media or seen on television, videos, or motion pictures.

Any reference to Disney, which was not part of the investigation, is deemed to be common knowledge or can be researched in public records including the Internet, trial transcripts and trial exhibits.

Forward

I grew up in a 970-square-foot house in Austin, Texas, with my parents and three siblings. Sunday nights were a big event for us because it was family television night. After my two older brothers and I played sports all day with our neighborhood friends, we came home to a hot meal cooked by my mother. After dinner, we sprawled across our living room floor in front of our three-channel Zenith television and watched Mutual of Omaha's Wild Kingdom, AND THEN, The Wonderful World of Disney!

The Wonderful World of Disney began with a picture of Cinderella's glorious castle, triumphantly joyous music playing, spectacular fireworks exploding all around the castle, and Tinkerbell spreading her pixie dust. It was magical. Then the Disney show began. With no previews or teasers in the 1960s, you never knew what the show would be. Maybe an animated story, or something more adventurous like Old Yeller or Swiss Family Robinson.

Who would have thought that some of the life lessons I learned as a kid by watching Disney would come full circle and reappear in the form of a federal criminal case when I was ending my career as an FBI Agent. Some of the lessons I learned from watching Disney shows included the ability to distinguish between good and bad; traits found in everyone. From Mary Poppins, I learned every action had a consequence. From Cinderella, I learned the way you treat others sometimes determines the way you will be treated. From Lady and the Tramp, I learned the path of integrity can be difficult but always rewarding.

Now understand, this book really has nothing to do with Disney. In fact, until the government contacted them, Disney had no idea their name was being misused by conman Thomas Lucas, Jr. in a scheme to defraud hundreds of victims out of millions of dollars. Disney's part in this case was limited to three of their employees testifying at a criminal trial that Disney had no plans of building a theme park in North Texas. The Disney employees were only three witnesses in a case that involved numerous witnesses. All references to Disney came from witness testimony or evidence introduced at trial, including fraudulent documents generated by Lucas Jr. Once Disney was informed about the scheme, their executives, legal counsel, and employees were extremely accommodating with interviews and trial appearances in Sherman, Texas. Like the theme in their blockbuster film "The Lion King", the Disney folks did what needed to be done.

This story is about how a conman, who was described as a "liar all his life", concocted an elaborate scheme about Disney building a theme park in North Texas called Frontier Disney DFW (interchangeable with Frontier Disney). In the process, the conman endeared himself to his family's real estate company, participated in approximately 100 sales presentations (including an unconfirmed presentation to the Indianapolis Colts) and caused losses to investors of approximately $60 million dollars.

I have no idea if Thomas Lucas, Jr. was raised on Disney movies like I was. But if he was, he clearly ignored some of the lessons.

Regarding the investigation, I was the case agent and did most of the heavy lifting on the case. However, as with most cases in the FBI, no one agent conducts the entire case on his/her own. There were numerous other people who assisted and received minimal credit. The successful prosecution of Lucas Jr. was attributed to the assisting agents on my squad, support personnel in my office, several Assistant United States Attorneys, the State Department, and of course the numerous witnesses who testified at trial and fulfilled their civic duty to the United States.

Chapter One
"The Announcement"

In the 1960s, when Walt Disney was looking for land to purchase for Disney World, he had to keep the identity of Disney confidential. Walt Disney knew that if word got out that his company was purchasing land around Orlando, Florida, the prices would go through the roof, which would increase his costs. Therefore, Walt Disney used shell companies to secretly purchase the land. Some of the names of the shell companies included the Latin-American Development and Management Corp., Tomahawk Properties, and M.T. Lott ("empty lot")[1]. I understand that some of these shell company names might actually be used on buildings on Main Street in the Magic Kingdom theme park. To help hide the real estate purchases for the theme park, Disney World was initially referred to as "Project X".

By May 1965, 27,000 acres of land had been covertly purchased through various shell companies. Floridians were speculating as to the identity of the company secretly buying up all the land. Some thought it was Ford. Others thought it was McDonnell-Douglas and some others thought it was Boeing. A few mentioned the idea

---

[1] James Rufus Koren. (2016, April 9). How Disney used shell companies to start its Magic Kingdom. Retrieved from http://www.latimes.com/business/la-fi-disney-shell-companies-20160408-story.html

of Disney but when confronted with this speculation, Walt Disney denied the rumor. However, when several Disney employees were non-responsive with their answers when questioned about the land acquisitions, a local newspaper printed the story that Disney was behind the land purchases[2].

On November 15, 1965, Walt Disney went on television and made the announcement confirming that Disney was the mystery industry coming to central Florida[3]. Based on this announcement, land prices increased 1000%. To illustrate the land value increase in dollars, Walt Disney allegedly purchased his first parcel of land for $80 per acre and his last parcel of land for $80,000 per acre[4]. It is easy to see how the announcement of such a project by Disney could make landowners rich; and thus, investors who purchased land around the theme park rich, too.

Forty years later, a similar scenario would play out in Texas; or would it? This time the scenario would be created by a pitifully arrogant conman, and without the knowledge or authorization of anyone associated with Disney.

---

[2] Walt Disney World History 101 – "How to buy 27,000 acres of land and have no one notice". (2016, June 24). Retrieved from http://www.wdwradio.com/2005/02/wdw-history-101-how-to-buy-27000-acres-of-land-and-no-one-noticeq/

[3] The secret Florida land deal that became Walt Disney World. (2017, May 16). Retrieved from http://www.miamiherald.com/news/state/florida/article150733437.html

[4] Walt Disney World History 101 – "How to buy 27,000 acres of land and have no one notice". (2016, June 24). Retrieved from http://www.wdwradio.com/2005/02/wdw-history-101-how-to-buy-27000-acres-of-land-and-no-one-noticeq/

Chapter Two
"Takeover Bandits"

On November 4, 2004, a group of bank robbers appropriately referred to as the "Takeover Bandits" had just robbed another bank in Richardson, Texas. The Takeover Bandits were a violent group committing bank robberies in the Dallas, Texas metroplex. They entered banks with fully automatic AK-47 assault rifles and shot up the banks. They were credited with 60 robberies and numerous carjackings. They were known to wear body armor. They intimidated bank personnel and injured witnesses. Based on their past actions, they were clearly considered armed and dangerous; or in law enforcement language "A&D". The Takeover Bandits once beat a security guard so fiercely that the guard's ear detached from the side of his head. Their aggressive approach to robbing banks was unusual. Over my 25-year career, most of the bank robberies we saw were "Note Jobs". Note Jobs are bank robberies where the criminals go into a bank and pass a note to the teller. The note will say something as simple as "give me the money, I have a gun". Bank robbers know that when an actual firearm is displayed, their federal sentence will get them twenty years in prison. However, the Takeover Bandits did not care how long they spent in jail. They were willing to inflict pain and death on citizens without being provoked. Apprehending this gang was already a law enforcement priority; however, on this date, the Takeover Bandits took their violence to a new level.

After committing their latest bank robbery, three of the bank robbers headed north on State Highway 75 towards Plano, Texas. While en route, the Takeover Bandits were identified by an officer of the Richardson, Texas Police Department (RPD). The RPD officer called in the license plate of the vehicle and while doing so, the Takeover Bandits opened fire on him while on the highway. The dramatic chase, which played out on national media outlets and over the Internet, was on. Several RPD officers joined in the chase. Since the deadly assault on the RPD officer occurred on the Plano-Richardson border, it did not take long for the entire Plano, Texas Police Department (PPD) to join in the pursuit. By now, the Takeover Bandits had got off the congested highway and were frantically attempting to escape in the Plano neighborhoods. Hundreds of rounds had been fired by the Takeover Bandits, and five police vehicles were totaled.

Also, by this time the FBI SWAT team had been notified of the shootout and chase. The FBI has primary jurisdiction in the investigations of bank robberies because of the federally insured deposits. Local police departments are supportive of this jurisdiction because bank robbers get more prison time in the federal system. To ensure cooperation between the local police and the FBI, the FBI in Dallas has a bank robbery task force where most local police departments have an officer dedicated to the task force. The bank robbery task force had been trying to apprehend the Takeover Bandits for some time.

As a member of the FBI SWAT team, I assisted with the search for the Takeover Bandits. They had crashed their vehicle into a telephone pole and escaped on foot. The East Plano neighborhoods were buzzing with RPD officers, PPD officers, FBI agents and the Texas Rangers. However, they had escaped law enforcement once again.

Approximately two months later (January 2005), a confidential informant informed the FBI of the identity and the address of one of the Takeover Bandits. His name was Gerardo Ramirez[5]. The FBI SWAT team set up to apprehend Ramirez at his apartment complex in Mesquite, Texas.

We had two vans on scene. One van had six agents from our Gold Team in it including me and two of my best friends, Special Agent Darrell James and Special Agent Steve Kleinlein. We were designated as the assault team, which meant we were the ones who would put "hands-on" Ramirez. The other van contained operators from the Blue Team. This van was to be used to block Ramirez's escape by blocking his car once he parked.

Our plan was to allow Ramirez to park at his apartment and allow him to exit his car. The Gold Team would arrest Ramirez while he was walking from his car to his front door. By allowing Ramirez to exit his vehicle, we would be able to see whether he was carrying any assault rifles. While the Gold Team was making our approach to execute the arrest, the Blue Team would simultaneously use their van to block Ramirez's vehicle in the event he tried to run back to his vehicle and use it for his escape.

The plan seemed straight forward. However, you must always expect Murphy's Law to occur; that is, if something can go wrong, it usually does. The FBI is exceptionally good about ensuring the SWAT operators are mentally prepared to handle dangerously changing situations; "Adapt, improvise and overcome," words tattooed in your mind.

Our team had sat in the back of the van, in full gear, all afternoon. Even though it was January, it was unseasonably hot, even for Texas. Judging from the sweat dripping on the van's hot metal

---

[5] Some names in this book are fictional

floorboard, we must have dropped a few pounds. We could not run the air conditioning because that might draw Ramirez's attention to our parked van. There was plenty of time to go over the ops plan in your head, attempting to anticipate every contingency. At approximately 5:00 pm, a SWAT surveillance team member transmitted over the radio that Ramirez was entering the complex. We could see Ramirez from the crack in the van's partially opened back door. The intensity of the situation had amped up since we knew Ramirez had no respect for life. While focusing on the task at hand, I was telling myself, *do your job and don't let your teammates down.* Just prior to Special Agent James instructing us to execute our plan, he observed the second van jump the order. The Blue Team prematurely blocked Ramirez's tan Altima before Ramirez exited his vehicle. Special Agent James alerted us of the early action taken by the Blue Team and instructed us to execute the arrest.

We swiftly jumped out of the van's side door and back door, sprinting approximately 30 yards across the parking lot. By the time the Gold Team got to Ramirez, he was still in the car with the engine running. Special Agent James ripped open the door and attempted to grab Ramirez, but Ramirez immediately shifted the vehicle into reverse. When Ramirez saw he could not go backwards because of the blocking van, he shifted into drive and gunned the engine. The vehicle violently jumped the curb. However, one of the apartment buildings was in front of Ramirez, so he had nowhere to go except back towards our direction. When I saw Ramirez's vehicle fish-tail, and heard the revving of the engine, I realized Ramirez was now heading in our direction. Our SWAT Team was in a deadly force situation. We opened fire on Ramirez to prevent the loss of our lives and the lives of other agents protecting the perimeter. Ramirez was hit several times. Incidental to his wounds, Ramirez crashed into his own apartment unit. What were the chances of this?

Special Agent James took the lead on pulling the injured Ramirez from his vehicle and cuffing him. Special Agent Kleinlein, myself and a couple of other SWAT operators immediately established security on Ramirez's front door preparing for a "hard" entry. In simple terms, a "hard" entry involves violently breaching the door with a battering ram, strategically tossing a diversionary device into the premises and tactically entering the premises with controlled speed shouting "FBI" to identify ourselves, ready to neutralize any threat to you or your team. Since there were other Takeover Bandits who were still on the run, and since we had no intelligence whether they were in the apartment, we had to address the situation as if they were there. Ramirez's crashed vehicle caused a small child to exit the apartment. After confirming with the child there were no other children in the apartment and after removing the child to safety, we decided to go in. Within a couple of minutes of the crash, we tossed a diversionary device into the apartment and went in. Upon entering, the first thing we noticed was the smoking engine from the hood of Ramirez's tan Altima which had penetrated halfway into the living area of the apartment. The smell of radiator fluid consumed the apartment as we searched for other threats. We cleared the apartment but unfortunately, there were no other Takeover Bandits in the apartment. After the "All Clear" was given, I went outside and saw our team doctor administering medical aid to the gunshot Ramirez. Ramirez would go on to survive his wounds.

A few days later, the remaining two Takeover Bandits were arrested with less drama. I have since been asked if I was afraid during this situation. My response was "no" because of our training and because I had DJ (Special Agent James) leading the way, and Bag O' (Special Agent Kleinlein) covering my "six". I always had an unquestionable confidence in all the SWAT operators working beside me.

Chapter Three
"Pinocchio's Larger Twin"

Plano, Texas is a suburban city 25 miles north of downtown Dallas. The population was approximately 220,000 in 1998. It was considered, and to some extent, is still considered an affluent city. The city is inundated with parks and trails for youth sports and folks who love the outdoors. It has been on many lists as one of America's top cities to live in. Plano has been the home to some well-known sports celebrities such as NFL players Troy Aikman, Deion Sanders, Drew Pearson, Daryl "Moose" Johnston, and others. There are a lot of gated neighborhoods with big, expensive houses and Plano was viewed as a city for 'new money'. It has been the home of many corporate headquarters such as Frito-Lay, Electronic Data Services, and JC Penny to name a few. Just east of the Plano city limits is Southfork Ranch, JR Ewing's TV home on the blockbuster drama, "Dallas". With the affluent reputation came the unarguable reality that Plano was a place where individuals were always trying to "keep up with the Joneses".

In the late summer of 1993, the city gained national media recognition when a 7-year-old girl was abducted from one of the many soccer fields in Plano during a Labor Day Weekend soccer tournament. This young angel was found murdered the next day. For all the pain this tragedy caused the little girl's family and the nightmares that haunt law enforcement officers, some good came out of it. Texas established a law known as Ashley's Law. This law was enacted to protect children from sexual predators.

In 1996, Plano received more national media coverage when numerous teenage kids were overdosing on Chiva. Chiva is black tar heroin. The overdoses occurred throughout Plano. Plano thus became known as a city with too much money and not enough supervision. There was an insurmountable pressure to excel academically, athletically, and socially. The pressure to excel socially and keep up with the Joneses was part of Thomas Lucas Jr.'s problem.

In 1998, Lucas Jr. was a senior at Plano Senior High School (PSHS), in Plano. The school was a football powerhouse in the late 1970s and early 1980s. Lucas Jr. had played on the football team in 1998.

As a senior in high school, Lucas Jr. appeared to have a normal life. Apart from playing football, he had a girlfriend, and hung out with friends. Lucas Jr. was an 18-year-old kid, about 5 feet, 9 inches tall, and was overweight. He suffered from severe migraines which caused him to frequently miss school. Lucas Jr.'s girlfriend, Jennifer Stark[6], did not know if Lucas Jr. graduated with their class because he missed so much school.

Lucas Jr. was described by his circle of friends as "a liar", "someone who had a problem telling the truth", and "someone who had the reputation of being full of shit"; however, his friends believed he was harmless. Lucas Jr.'s friends took his lies with a grain of salt and believed he was just trying to fit in. His friends rationalized Lucas Jr.'s bragging as someone just dreaming of having the perception of success. He would say and do anything to

---

[6] Fictional name.

make this dream come true. Texas refers to people such as this as "all hat, no cattle."

On one occasion, Stark was invited to a hockey game by Lucas Jr. The Dallas Stars were competing for the National Hockey League's Stanley Cup and Lucas Jr. informed Stark that he had scored two tickets to the next playoff game. Stark was excited to go. On game day, Stark dressed in her green Dallas Stars' jersey and excitedly waited for Lucas Jr. to pick her up. She was impatiently awaiting by her front door when Lucas Jr. pulled into her driveway. When Stark eagerly bounced into the car, Lucas Jr. asked if "Jeff" had delivered the tickets to her. Stark confusingly thought to herself why in the world would someone she did not know deliver the tickets to her instead of Lucas Jr? He then went on with a ridiculous explanation about how "Jeff" was supposed to stop by Stark's house and drop off the hockey tickets. Stark immediately realized this was just another one of Lucas Jr.'s lies, and that there were never any hockey tickets. Unsurprisingly, Stark and Lucas Jr. did not attend the hockey game.

Close friends of Lucas Jr. told a story about *his* Mustang Cobra. Lucas Jr. bragged to his friends how he had bought a hot new Mustang Cobra. He would continuously brag about it. However, nobody ever saw it. When a friend went to his house and noticed the obvious absence of the Mustang Cobra, Lucas Jr. said a family member was borrowing it. Eventually, Lucas Jr. told his friends he sold the vehicle because he could not afford the automobile insurance on it. Lucas Jr.'s friends said this was typical of the kinds of lies Lucas Jr. would tell. He would tell one lie that he knew he would be called on someday, and when he was called on it, he covered the first lie with another one. I have sat across the table from many white-collar criminals who did this. I have even assisted in some interviews where the case agent would tell the defendant "if you're going to lie to us, just leave." When I conducted the interview, I did not mind the sociopath who kept telling lies upon lies. The more I could get a defendant to talk, the more information he/she would give me to disprove; and disproving a 'fact' was sometimes easier than *proving* the fact. Also, the lies told by the defendant always played well for a jury at trial. When the case agent testified at trial about the lies told by a defendant, the defendant usually could not refute them because most defense attorneys do not want their client testifying. However, if by chance, the defendant does testify to the same set of circumstances where he previously lied, then the obvious question by the prosecutor is "are you lying now or were you lying then?"

Another friend of Lucas Jr. named Bob Pressley[7] had grown up with Lucas Jr. They played football together, double dated to Homecoming, and double dated to the Prom. Pressley abruptly ended his friendship with Lucas Jr. due to Lucas Jr. being a habitual liar. Pressley worked at a local video store with him during and after high school. One day, Lucas Jr. showed up late to work while they were extremely busy. Pressley asked Lucas Jr. why he was late. Lucas Jr. responded he had to spend some time with his mother because she had stage 4 cancer. According to Lucas Jr., she was going to die within the next 90 days. Pressley sorrowfully accepted Lucas Jr.'s explanation and went back to work. However, the next time Pressley was at Lucas Jr.'s house, he saw Mrs. Lucas. Pressley went over to her, gave her a hug, and told her how sorry he was to hear of her terminal illness. Pressley said Mrs. Lucas looked at him as if he had sprouted a third eye. She asked what the heck was wrong with him and informed Pressley she was not sick, nor was she dying.

---

[7] Fictional name

11

Despite his constant lies, Lucas Jr.'s friends considered him to be an extremely intelligent person who was exceptionally competent with computers. He always had the best and most expensive software and equipment. One friend who was currently in the computer software industry said he had seen Lucas Jr. do things on his computer that a layman would have no idea how to do. This was relevant because in the 2000s, committing fraud using the computer was not as easy as it is today. The software was not as advanced.

Between 2002 and 2004, Lucas Jr. worked for his father and his uncle, Chip Lucas[8] (Uncle Chip), at the Harry B. Lucas Company. For reference purposes, the Harry B. Lucas Company, the Lucas Real Estate Company, and Harry B. Lucas Management Trust are collectively referred to as HBLCO. In 2004, Lucas Jr. was 24-years old and was paid $1,000-$2,000 per month for not really doing anything. Uncle Chip described Lucas Jr. as a bright kid who lacked motivation. Lucas Jr. never took an interest in the real estate business. He was described as more of an Internet Technology (IT) guy. Basically, he fixed the computers in the office when there were problems. Uncle Chip considered Lucas Jr. nothing more than a "go-fer" (someone who would "go for" things or run errands) for HBLCO.

In early 2005, Uncle Chip claimed he fired Lucas Jr. However, Lucas Jr.'s father disagreed that he was fired. His father described the situation as the company having financial problems, so they just stopped paying Lucas Jr. This certainly had me scratching my head trying to figure out what the difference was. Either way it was phrased, Lucas Jr. was not relevant to the overall future of the HBLCO. For his own family having to terminate his employment,

---

[8] Fictional name

Lucas Jr. must have felt immensely unimportant and inadequate. He was a person who had a hard time fitting in with friends, and now his own family was tossing him aside.

In 2008, just prior to his ten-year reunion at Plano Senior High School, Lucas Jr. posted on his MySpace page a photo of him standing by a red Ferrari. MySpace was a social media application, which was a sort of predecessor to Facebook. The photo and the caption made it appear that the Ferrari was his, which was his intention. I learned much later that the photo of the red Ferrari was fake. Lucas Jr. also represented on the MySpace page that he was the president of the Lucas Real Estate Company. This was during the time Lucas Jr. was committing fraud. He had posted this information to impress his classmates. Again, Lucas Jr. was continuing his lies to "keep up with the Joneses".

By the time I was assigned this case and delved into Lucas Jr.'s past, I was referring to him as Pinocchio's larger twin because of all the lies he told throughout his life. When Lucas Jr. started his scheme in 2005, he was 25 years' old. By the time I started my investigation in 2012, Lucas Jr. was 32, and still living at home.

Chapter Four
"Bachelor Party"

In early 2005, the FBI had just arrested members of one of the most violent bank robbery gangs in Dallas history and Lucas Jr. had just been fired by his Uncle Chip from HBLCO. He must have felt like an enormous disappointment to his family. Attempting to save his job, Lucas Jr. concocted an unbelievable story. He told his Uncle Chip he heard some big, well-known company was coming to North Texas. This unknown company was apparently secretly buying land in the area. However, the vagueness of the information was not enough to save Lucas Jr.'s job. Uncle Chip told him that if he could determine the identity of the company buying the land, then maybe they could do something with the information. However, until then, it was good-bye.

In June 2005, Lucas Jr. attended a bachelor party in Austin, Texas for an old high-school friend, Mitchell Robinson[9]. Robinson had gone on to become a doctor in Austin, Texas which is located approximately three and a half hours south of Plano. Austin is an oasis located in the heart of Texas. It is surrounded by rolling hills, and boasts of cold lakes, live music and great bar-b-q. It was also the city in which my siblings and I grew up. When I was in elementary school and my older brothers were in junior high

---

[9] Fictional name

(middle school), we used to sell soft drinks at the University of Texas Longhorn football games to make some spending money. I was always glad when an investigation took me home.

Lucas Jr. and Dr. Robinson had attended high school together in Plano, Texas. The attendees of the bachelor party included approximately twelve to fifteen individuals comprised of Dr. Robinson's high-school friends and his fraternity brothers from the University of Texas. This was a weekend event in which the attendees stayed at a genuinely nice hotel in the middle of Austin overlooking beautiful Town Lake.

The bachelor party included the usual debauchery experienced at these types of events, exotic strippers and a lot of drinking. Friday night started at a local strip club called PTAX[10], which was located on the south side of town. On Saturday, the guys drove south of San Marcos, Texas to go tubing down the pleasantly cool Guadalupe River. San Marcos is located approximately 35 minutes south of Austin. The Guadalupe River attracts more than a million young adults each summer for tubing, sunbathing and drinking. That Saturday night, strippers were hired from one of the local strip clubs to come to the party's spacious hotel room to dance.

Amidst all the drinking, hollering, and dancing by scantily clad women, Lucas Jr. thought it would be a good idea to discuss business. He asked his friend, Brian Mattingly[11], whether he had heard that Disney was building a theme park in North Texas. Lucas Jr. falsely claimed that the owner of the Dallas Cowboys had just sold a piece of land to Disney. The land was located at the top of the

---

[10] Fictional name

[11] Fictional name

Dallas North Tollway in Celina, Texas[12]. Lucas Jr. told Mattingly that he (Lucas Jr.) was trying to get investors in the deal because his family's real estate company was involved.

Lucas Jr.'s intent by bringing up Disney, was to plant a seed in a witness's mind. Remember that when Lucas Jr. was being terminated by his Uncle Chip a couple of months prior to the bachelor party, he did not have any idea of the name of the fictional company allegedly buying land in North Texas. Therefore, he made up the scenario and identified the company as Disney. The bachelor party in Austin, Texas served as Lucas Jr.'s birthing place for his web of deceit.

Lucas Jr. did not return to Dallas until approximately midnight that Sunday night. By dawn on Monday morning, he was rushing to HBLCO. He burst into his father's office where Uncle Chip was present and shouted, "It's Disney!" Lucas Jr. informed his father and uncle that he had reunited with a lifelong friend at the bachelor party who worked for Disney, and who provided him with the confidential information that Disney was buying land in North Texas. It was quite a coincidence that Lucas Jr. had heard of a big company buying land in North Texas and someone at the bachelor party knew the identity of the company.

Lucas Jr. boldly vouched for the integrity of the source and informed his Uncle Chip that his friend had secretly shown him (Lucas Jr.) a paystub from Disney and a Disney employee identification badge. Lucas Jr. and Uncle Chip discussed the potential for making a lot of money if they could determine the exact location of the land Disney was purchasing. If this information could be obtained, they could solicit investors to buy the land surrounding

---

[12] Celina, Texas is located approximately 50 miles north of Dallas, Texas.

the theme park. When this information went public, they stood to make a lot of money (as happened after the announcement of Disney World back in 1965). Uncle Chip pressed Lucas Jr. to get more information from his unnamed Disney source. Lucas Jr. agreed but vowed never to disclose the name of his source. Lucas Jr. conveyed that the purpose of the source's anonymity was so the source would not be fired by Disney. The real purpose, of course, was because there was no Disney source, so Lucas Jr. had to remain in control of the whole situation. He said his Disney source did not want payment. The source was just trying to help a friend make some money. Uncle Chip agreed to pay Lucas Jr. one percent of each deal that closed and an additional one percent to wine and dine the Disney source so the source would continue to provide additional information.

Between June 2005 and October 2005, Uncle Chip pressured Lucas Jr. about the Disney theme park. Uncle Chip wanted more information and wanted to know the name of Lucas Jr.'s Disney source. Lucas Jr. subsequently provided the name of the Disney source as Garrett Singleton[13], who was employed by the Excalibur Management Group[14]. Lucas Jr. explained that the Excalibur Management Group was the company hired by Disney to secretly buy land around Celina, Texas (a la Disney World). While talking to his Uncle Chip, Lucas Jr. referenced the history of how Disney World was started. Now a reasonable person might ask if the Disney source worked for Excalibur Management Group, then how does this person have a check stub or employee identification badge from Disney? The answer may have been as simple as the greedy do not weigh themselves down with details, or maybe they just did not care.

---

[13] Fictional name

[14] Fictional name

Uncle Chip realized that sophisticated investors would not invest their money on the word of a 25-year-old "go-fer". He told Lucas Jr. that they needed proof that Disney was legitimately planning to build a theme park in North Texas. In October 2005, Lucas Jr. concocted an email, allegedly written by Mr. Singleton and addressed to Lucas Jr.'s email address. Lucas Jr. forwarded the email to Uncle Chip. The email contained the following attached documents:

A copy of a letter dated May 21, 2005, from Ken Webb[15], Vice President, Excalibur Management Group to Jay Rasulo regarding the new entrance to the "King Ranch Project". Rasulo was identified as the Chairman of Walt Disney Parks and Resorts. The King Ranch Project was changed to Frontier Disney DFW a few months later. Note that the name of the "King Ranch Project" was similar to the reference of "Project X" for Disney World. I presumed the reference to projects was to fool investors or anyone else who might research the Internet for similarities between the secret purchases of real estate by Disney.

The verbatim text of the letter will be discussed later. However, the purpose of the letter was to create the appearance that Excalibur Management Group was informing executive management at Disney that land acquisitions for the theme park were 98% complete. The letter also referenced the best place for the theme park's entrance; and that "Garret", "George" and Webb would be flying to Hong Kong to assist with the opening of Hong Kong Disneyland[16].

---

[15] Fictional name

[16] Hong Kong Disneyland opened in September 2005.

A copy of a letter dated August 15, 2005, from Jay Rasulo, "President", Walt Disney Parks and Resorts, to the Excalibur Management Team naming the Disney executive who would oversee the daily operations of Frontier Disney DFW. The wording of this letter will also be discussed later.

A colored photocopy of a Preliminary Concept Plan for Frontier Disney DFW. On the right side of the plan there was a photo of Mickey Mouse hovering over Cinderella's castle with the phrase Disney Frontier DFW. This was the logo for Frontier Disney DFW. Underneath the logo, there was a picture of a family on the main street of the theme park. On the right side of the street was a western-style covered wagon. The concept plan also reflected the architecture firm designing the park as Law Kingdon (spelled correctly). On the left side of the Preliminary Concept Plan was an aerial map outlining the boundaries of the theme park. The aerial map also depicted the airport which would be built southwest of the park's borders.

Lucas Jr. had just gone from a fired employee to king of the mountain. Some might even sarcastically state "he went from zero to hero in no time flat", which were lyrics in one of the songs from Disney's animated hit movie "Hercules".

Chapter Five
"The Announcement Revisited"

In late 2005, forty years after the Disney World theme park was announced, Uncle Chip approached Sean Hartman[17] about an investment opportunity that could make Hartman a lot of money. Uncle Chip claimed that his nephew, Lucas Jr., had a reliable inside source at Disney, who provided Lucas Jr. secret information that Disney was planning to build a theme park in North Texas. The theme park would be vastly similar to Disney World in Orlando, Florida. Uncle Chip told Hartman that since he knew the theme park's location, his company was buying the land surrounding the proposed theme park prior to Disney making their announcement about the theme park. Uncle Chip stated that by purchasing the land now, when Disney made their announcement, the land purchased by HBLCO and their investors would skyrocket in value.

The investment could be made in one of two ways. One way was to purchase the land outright. This method would make the investors landowners. Therefore, if Disney did not build the theme park, at least, the investors would have real estate collateralizing their investment. The second way was the option to purchase the land (option contracts) by pooling their money with other investors to purchase the option contracts through various entities or

---

[17] Fictional name

joint ventures. The investors entered into option contracts to purchase specific parcels of land at a specified price, but only for a limited time. The option contracts were drafted to expire shortly after the pending Disney announcement was to be made. This method allowed the investors to place money in escrow to tie up the land. Once the announcement of Disney's intentions to build the theme park was public, the value of the land surrounding the theme park would increase. Since the investors had locked in their purchase price at a lower price, they stood to make a significant profit from the margin between their lower contracted price and the future inflated price. The problem with the option contracts was that the landowner or seller still owned the land. If the contract to purchase the land did not close within a specified number of days, then the investors would lose their escrow money, unless they paid additional money to extend the duration of the contract.

Unbeknownst to Hartman, the investment opportunity was made to him just a few months after Lucas Jr. had returned from his friend's bachelor party in Austin where he allegedly obtained the Disney information. Uncle Chip informed Hartman that Disney was in the process of buying land through a company called Excalibur Management Group so they could open a theme park in North Texas. The Excalibur Management Group was being used in a similar fashion to how the shell companies were used to acquire land for Disney World in 1965. Uncle Chip conveyed how the information about the Disney theme park came from a secret source who was a lifelong friend of Lucas Jr. and who worked at Disney. Neither Hartman nor the future investors were told that Lucas Jr. "obtained" the Disney information while drinking and watching nude women dance at a bachelor party. Hartman expressed an interest but he did not want to inflate land values by buying land and messing up anything Disney was doing.

In February 2006, Uncle Chip re-approached Hartman and told him that Disney had acquired all the land they needed to build the theme park. This information had come from Lucas Jr. Uncle Chip stressed that the land bought around the proposed theme park would increase in value upon the announcement of the Disney theme park. Hartman was shown the two letters written in 2005 exchanged between Jay Rasulo, "President" of Disney Parks and Resorts, and Ken Webb, Excalibur Management Group. Uncle Chip pointed out to Hartman that the land necessary to build the theme park had been acquired and Disney was ready to move on building the theme park. Hartman was then reassured that since Disney had acquired all the land they needed, there was no problem with investing in the surrounding land because this would no longer negatively impact anything related to Disney.

Uncle Chip further informed Hartman that Disney intended to make the announcement about their North Texas theme park on Thanksgiving Day during the Dallas Cowboy football game. Between February 2006 and November 23, 2006, Uncle Chip solicited several investors to purchase a particular parcel of land located across the street from the alleged entrance of the theme park. Hartman was an attorney working for a big law firm so he knew several people with money who would also be interested in investing.

Around September 2006, Hartman wanted some questions answered about the Disney deal. He contacted Uncle Chip, who had to defer to Lucas Jr. Attempting to avoid answering questions, Lucas Jr. sent an email to Uncle Chip and Mark Emerson reporting his Disney source was out of the country and could not be contacted. Thanksgiving Day 2006 was quickly approaching so the investors knew they had to get their money in to purchase the land. In early November 2006, Hartman personally invested $300,000 of a $7 million purchase of 105 acres of land. The other members of the limited liability company came up with the additional $6.7 million.

Thanksgiving Day 2006 finally arrived. The Dallas Cowboys trampled the Tampa Bay Buccaneers 38-10 after Quarterback Tony Romo threw for five touchdowns. However, Disney did not make the announcement during the game. Uncle Chip embarrassingly explained to Hartman and the other investors that the Thanksgiving Day game was only a "soft" date for the announcement. Uncle Chip explained that Lucas Jr. had talked to his Disney source, and according to the Disney source, the "hard" date for the announcement would be during halftime of the 2007 Super Bowl. Responses to Hartman and the other investors' questions were delayed for a couple of months.

On February 4, 2007, several investors met with Uncle Chip, Lucas Jr., and Mark Emerson at one of the investor's house to watch the Super Bowl and celebrate the announcement. Emerson was a salesman who had recently been hired by HBLCO. There was a lot of drinking and a Mickey Mouse shaped cake at the Super Bowl party. Naturally, the announcement was not made at halftime as anticipated. Lucas Jr. took his laptop and secretly went into the back bedroom. He emerged in the fourth quarter and notified the investors of an unexpected crisis. While in the bedroom, Lucas Jr. had concocted a blog reflecting the Disney theme park had been delayed. Lucas Jr. said his Disney source had contacted him and explained that Disney did not make the announcement because they needed more land. This did not make sense to Hartman because Uncle Chip had guaranteed him that Disney had all the land they needed, which was the reason Hartman had invested in the first place. Uncle Chip explained there was also a problem with some of the deeds, according to the Disney source.

The new announcement date was scheduled for the 2008 Super Bowl, according to the Disney source. Uncle Chip informed the investors that over the next year, Disney should be able to acquire the land necessary, and resolve all deed issues.

I would subsequently hear about this party from several investors. I can only imagine the stress Lucas Jr. must have been feeling trying to come up with a reason for the delayed announcement. Lucas Jr. had just bought himself another year to avoid telling the truth.

Over the next year, hundreds of investors would invest millions of dollars based on the misrepresentations made and/or facilitated by Lucas Jr.

Everything was tied to the announcement date; a date that would never come.

Since Hartman was an attorney, he was one of the first to sue Lucas Jr. and HBLCO. This lawsuit would prove significantly helpful when the FBI got involved in 2012.

Chapter Six
"Reflections"

Staring out of the seventh-floor window of the FBI office in Frisco, Texas, I reflected on my career as I prepared to go to yet another retirement lunch for a Special Agent who had dedicated his life to public service. It had been over twenty-two years since I graduated from the FBI Academy in Quantico, Virginia. I smiled when I recalled how our trainer, Special Agent Bob Rogers, who was a salty, retired Marine, laughed at us doing push-ups in the freezing, muddy tank trails on the Marine Corp Base at Quantico. So too the memories of the 'Yellow Brick Road' and the 'Belly of the Beast', both being events that physically challenged new agents. Pushing your body to its physical limits seemed less difficult when you were doing it with people you trusted and respected. The exhausting physical challenges almost seemed fun.

I reflected on the relationships I made over the years such as my close friendships with Special Agent Darrell James and Special Agent Steve Kleinlein, two great agents, and fellow SWAT operators. I referred to Special Agent James as "DJ" or "Deej". DJ is a US Marine (once a Marine, always a Marine), a natural leader, and a proud alumnus of the University of Georgia. We saw eye-to-eye on many issues; however, one of our rare disagreements was who came from the better conference—Big XII or SEC. I cannot count the number of lunches I lost to DJ for a Big XII team losing to an SEC team. I referred to Special Agent Kleinlein as Stevie "Bag O' Donuts". I gave this nickname to him early in our career because when we were new agents working on the same squad, he would come to the office every morning with a packet of convenience-store, white-powdered donuts for his breakfast. "Stevie Bag O' Donuts" was later shortened to "Bag O". Bag O' and I would have contests on who was the best shot on the SWAT team. The loser owed the winner a six-pack of the winner's favorite beverage. When Bag O' transferred out of the Dallas Division, I gave him a couple of cases of Diet Coke as a down payment of what I owed him over the years. Without a doubt, Bag O' was the best shot on the SWAT team.

In the late fall of 1990, I had left my job as a bank examiner working for the Office of the Comptroller of the Currency (OCC). The OCC was an agency under the United States Department of Treasury. This agency was responsible for the regulation of all national banks in the United States. I was hired by the FBI under the Financial Institutions Reform, Recovery, and Enforcement Act (FIRREA) of 1989. FIRREA was a United States federal law enacted because of the savings and loan debacle of the 1980s. During the 1980s and continuing into the early 1990s, approximately one-third of the savings and loan associations across America failed. The reason for the failures had to do with several factors including unsound financial liberties taken as a result of deregulation. However, I learned from my participation in the actual arena, it was generally due to executive management using deregulation to promote unsound and unsafe real estate lending. Executive management of financial institutions were generating loans based on quantity rather than quality because numerous loans gave the appearance of growth. When a financial institution has unsound lending practices, growth is not always a good thing. Coupled with bonuses for management being tied to the number of loans extended created an environment for potential fraud. This was evident in the 1980s with the savings and loan scandal, and it partially assisted with the mortgage fraud scandal in 2006-2008.

The liberal lending practices of the financial institutions' funds resulted in a small percentage of loan officers either cutting corners to aggressively make loans, or openly committing fraud to make loans. Why? Because bonuses were tied to the quantity of loans and the growth of the institution. In addition to the employees of the financial institutions committing fraud, outside players conspired with the employees to commit fraud. Some of these players included land developers, appraisers, escrow officers, fee attorneys, straw borrowers, and other opportunists.

FIRREA created several agencies, including the Resolution Trust Corporation which was charged with closing numerous savings associations that were declared insolvent and handling their assets. FIRREA created the Office of Thrift Supervision, an agency of the Department of Treasury, which regulated savings associations. More importantly, FIRREA facilitated the hiring of several hundred new FBI agents with financial backgrounds, and I was fortunate enough to be amongst them. The idea was to assign this new group of agents to FBI squads who would address the fraud occurring within financial institutions across the United States.

My training at Quantico was a sixteen-week program. I was part of New Agent Class (NAC) 91-1. This number referred to the first class to graduate in 1991. During our time at Quantico, we successfully completed the four areas of training for new agents: physical fitness; firearms; academics; and practical applications. After completing my sixteen-week training at Quantico, I was assigned to the Dallas Field Office of the FBI. Because of my financial background, I was assigned to the Bank Fraud squad. I was successful in investigating numerous interesting cases, such as the "Contra Files-Ranch Days" case; and the "Sovereign Cherokee Nation" case. The Contra Files-Ranch Days case was the unofficial name I gave to a case where the Chief Executive Officer (CEO) and the president of Lone Star National Bank directed their young loan officers to appear at the bank on the weekend before the bank examiners were to commence a bank examination. The CEO and the president instructed their employees to purge all negative documents from the loan files that would reflect poorly on the loan, such as bankruptcy filings, past due notices, deficient appraisals, side agreements, etc. All the negative documents were either shredded or placed in secret files, which I labeled the contra files because of the Iran-Contra affair that played out in the late 1980s. The CEO did not want the bank examiners to see the documents because the documents would negatively impact the financial condition of the bank. Such documents would increase loan losses, which would deplete capital and eventually cause insolvency. The CEO was also forcing his young, male, loan officers to go to his ranch near Corinth, Texas every other Thursday to pick up rocks, mend fences and herd livestock. To listen to the young loan officers describe the labor they did at the ranch was sadly humorous. A good question was, why the young loan officers agreed to participate in such illegal and demeaning behavior? It was due to the manipulation by the CEO. The CEO would pay his young loan officers a high salary; as much as $15,000-$20,000 more than young bank officers at other banks. The CEO would also harassingly encourage his young officers to buy big houses (which had big mortgages) and have children. By doing this, the young loan offices could not afford to quit and get another high-paying bank job that would pay their large mortgage and support the costs of raising children. I cannot count the number of times I have asked a white-collar subject, "so you had the choice to break the law or quit your job, and you chose to break the law?" Money is a huge motivator.

The "Sovereign Cherokee Nation" case was the unofficial name I gave a case where a Canadian, non-Native American, proclaimed himself to be the "chief" of the Sovereign Cherokee Nation. The location of this Nation was a small strip of land located in the middle of the Rio Grande between the United States and Mexico. Basically, it was a patch of mud. The "chief" said their laws authorized them to generate bogus Certificates of Deposit (CD) and pledge them towards legitimate bank loans. The way this worked was the "chief" went to a Dallas area bank and got a $100,000 loan. The "chief" pledged the $100,000 bogus CD against the loan. When the loan matured and did not payoff, the bank attempted to redeem the CD; however, since it was bogus, there was no place to redeem it. I have always wondered what was more humorous—the "chief" creating his own country and laws, or the banks that willingly and eagerly accepted the CDs as collateral. The lack of due diligence conducted by some financial institutions would make any reasonable person shake his head. But like I said, money is a huge motivator, for criminals as well as victims.

After completing my fourth year in the Bureau, I decided to try-out for the SWAT team. I had demonstrated my ability to successfully investigate white-collar crime cases. Now, I wanted a different challenge. I was selected to the team and completed eleven years with the SWAT team. The SWAT training and missions broke up the mundane work of going through voluminous boxes of documents associated with white-collar crime cases. SWAT missions included arresting some definitively violent criminals such as murderers, kidnappers, bank robbers, violent drug distributors and others who preyed on the innocent. I have since been asked which cases presented the bigger challenge, investigating violent criminals or investigating white-collar criminals. My answer is always the same. When you conduct interviews of violent criminals, you will always be the smartest person in the room. However, when you conduct interviews of white-collar criminals, you are rarely the smartest person in the room. Hands down, white-collar criminal investigations were always more challenging.

After completing four years in the Dallas Field Office, I transferred to the Plano Resident Agency, which subsequently became the Frisco Resident Agency when our office moved to Frisco, Texas. The FBI refers to a Resident Agency as an RA. RAs are small satellite offices of the main Field Office. There are 56 FBI Field Offices located in the United States and Puerto Rico, and each field office has RAs. RAs vary in size depending on the population of the territory they cover. The Frisco RA was located about twenty miles north of Dallas, which is considered quite close to have an RA. In fact, each of the eight Special Agents-in-Charge (SACs) who came to Dallas over the span of my career wanted to close the Frisco RA. The SACs all believed having an RA in such close proximity to the main office was a waste of money. However, once the SACs saw the successful prosecutions coming out of the Frisco RA, every SAC backed off their idea of shutting it down. When I began my work in the RA, we had an extremely limited number of agents assigned to the office. By the time I retired, the Frisco RA had three squads. It was considered a garden spot among the other RAs assigned to Dallas because of its close proximity to the main office and because of the relationship the agents had with the federal prosecutors at the United States Attorney's Office. The RA investigated white-collar cases, terrorism cases, and violent crime/drug cases in the Eastern District of Texas (EDTX) and the Northern District of Texas (NDTX). This was relevant because the district where the overt criminal act(s) is/are committed determined where the defendant of a case was prosecuted. Honestly, I felt the Assistant US Attorneys (AUSA) were more aggressive in the EDTX than in the NDTX. In my biased opinion, the AUSAs in the EDTX knew how to apply the law and were not afraid to make an argument in court.

Chapter Seven
"Feeling Dumber"

To his friends, Special Agent John Skillestad was known as Skilly. Skilly graduated from the FBI Academy in Quantico, Virginia, in December 1990, one month after I started at the Academy. He had a law degree from Loyola University, which made him desirable to the Bureau. The old Bureau loved lawyers and accountants. He was assigned to the Dallas Field Office out of Quantico, where he cut his teeth on chasing fugitives as part of the Violent Crime Squad. Several years later, Skilly transferred to the Frisco RA. He was the sole agent responsible for investigating violent crimes in the four-county area covered by the RA. Violent crime investigations within the Frisco office included bank robberies, fugitives, and anything not considered white-collar crime, terrorism, or drugs. Two of the counties included Collin County, and Denton County, which were both located in the Eastern District of Texas. Collin County was an affluent area and was considered one of the fastest growing counties in the United States between 2006 and 2015. This rapid growth made the county ripe for fraud and other criminal activity. Where there is money, there is always someone trying to steal it, either with the pen or the gun.

Skilly was an extremely likeable person. He loved sports and was an avid New Orleans Saints fan. If you were lucky enough to be considered one of his friends, then there was nothing he would not do for you. He was always quick to tell a "dad" joke and quick to laugh. Usually, he was the only one laughing. He was also an easy target to poke fun at because of his good sense of humor. I cannot count the number of times I jokingly told Skilly that every time I had a conversation with him, I would leave the conversation feeling dumber. To keep Skilly humble, I liked to remind him that all the money he spent on law school was wasted. My explanation was that although I was just an average student with no law degree, he and I had the same job and made the same amount of money. Despite the jokes, he was someone I respected and someone from whom I sought advice on numerous occasions. In fact, I have often thought that if anything bad had ever happened to my family such as a kidnapping; Skilly, DJ and Bag O would be the agents I would want assigned to the case. There were many other good agents in the Dallas Division, but I have spent too many long, hot days and wet, cold nights chasing criminals with these three guys. All three epitomize the Winston Churchill quote, "Never, ever, ever give up". Americans may never know the name of these three agents but they should sleep better knowing their character is representative of most street agents.

After finishing the retirement lunch at La Hacienda Ranch, Skilly asked me to help him with a lead originating from the FBI's Detroit Field Office. A lead is an official request made by one field office of the FBI (originating office) to have another field office of the FBI (lead office) complete a specific investigative task to assist with the case of the originating office. Any field office can be the originating office or the lead office. The specific investigative task is usually a request to conduct an interview, serve a subpoena, execute a search warrant, or execute an arrest warrant.

On the way to cover the Detroit lead, Skilly briefed me on the Detroit case. FBI-Detroit requested he interview the ex-wife of Terrence "T-Bone" Bonham[18]. T-Bone was a member of the Log Cabin Gang out of Detroit. The Log Cabin Gang was a violent group of thugs controlling a neighborhood in Detroit. T-Bone was wanted on a UFAP warrant. UFAP is an acronym for Unlawful Flight to Avoid Prosecution. The FBI provides assistance to local law enforcement agencies across the US and abroad in apprehending fugitives on UFAP warrants. Simply put, T-Bone was wanted for murder and was on the run. The Detroit Field Office was attempting to develop leads regarding T-Bone's whereabouts. According to the Detroit lead, which had been on Skilly's desk for a couple of months, T-Bone and the ex-wife had not spoken in years. Skilly also informed me there was no chance of T-Bone being at his ex-wife's residence. However, since T-Bone's daughter was graduating high school the coming weekend, Skilly was playing a hunch that T-Bone might want to see his only daughter graduate high school. I jokingly asked Skilly that if there was no chance of T-Bone being there, then why did he need me? In Skilly's defense, an agent never covers a lead like this alone. I think Skilly asked me to assist with the lead because of our trust in one another, because of my experience with high-risk arrests, because we made each other laugh, and since I worked white collar crimes; he sarcastically presumed I had nothing more exciting to do.

Skilly and I located the ex-wife's house in Plano, Texas. We ran the license plate of the blue Toyota Corolla parked in the driveway, which came back to the T-Bone's ex-wife. Upon knocking on the door of the two-story brick house, a female who identified herself as a friend of the ex-wife answered the door. The friend

---

[18] Fictional name.

gave her name as Sheila Jackson[19]. Jackson was petite and dressed in a house coat, which seemed unusual for an afternoon. After some persuasive comments by Skilly, Jackson agreed to talk to us and invited us into the living room, which was located just inside the front door. Skilly proceeded with the standard questions for attempting to locate a fugitive, such as "do you know him", "when was the last time you saw or talked to him", "what was the conversation about", "do you know where he is". Jackson was noticeably short with her answers and appeared a bit uneasy. I stopped the interview and quietly whispered to Jackson, "Is he here?" Shockingly, Jackson whispered "yes" and stated he was in the bedroom on the first floor. "Oh shit."

Skilly and I immediately pulled our service pistols. I took up a position behind an interior pillar so I could cover the hallway leading to the bedroom while Skilly attempted to obtain more information, such as was T-Bone armed and whether there was anyone else in the house. After several seconds of seemingly eternal silence, I loudly shouted in the direction of the back bedroom, "T-Bone, this is the FBI. I need you to slowly exit the bedroom with your hands up." There was no response, nor could we hear any shuffling or other movement. Knowing it is safer to have the bad guy come to the agents rather than the agents going in after the bad guy, especially giving this situation, we had a tactical decision to make. T-Bone knew we were there to arrest him, and he had time to develop a plan while we were interviewing Jackson. By bringing T-Bone to us, we could control the environment. However, after a short wait in the deafening silence, which felt like an eternity, we decided to go in after him. The idea of waiting for the subject to barricade himself or to get up enough nerve to confront us

---

[19] Fictional name

weighed on our minds, especially since Ms. Jackson did not know if T-Bone was armed.

Upon entering the bedroom there was nobody to be found. It is always alarming when you get to the room where the subject is supposed to be, and nobody is there. The only two hiding places in the small bedroom were under the bed, which was in the middle of the room or in the walk-in closet. Since the closet posed the most risk to us, we started for the closet. I was performing a tactical procedure known as "slicing the pie", which put me on the other side of the bed directly across from the closet entry. By "slicing the pie", I could slowly clear the open space of the closet. However, before we could take a few steps, T-Bone walked out of the closet in blue "Aladdin" type pants and a tee shirt. His hands were empty but he refused to put his hands above his head so we could inspect danger areas like his waistband. Skilly immediately grabbed T-Bone by the shirt with his free hand and pulled him onto the bed. I leaped across the bed onto T-Bone's back and cuffed him. Luckily for everyone involved, nobody was seriously injured.

After delivering T-Bone to the US Marshal's office, Skilly and I started back to the office. There was no way Skilly was getting off easy with this one. I looked at him and said, "No chance of him being there, huh? I think this is one of the few times where the violent criminal was smarter than the agent. Once again, I leave your presence feeling dumber." At least everyone was safe, and we had a good laugh.

The next day, Skilly would be on complaint duty. And once again, he would request my help.

Chapter Eight
"The Walk-In"

Complaint duty is a task alternated amongst the agents in the office. Each day, a different agent is assigned to receive and document information provided by the general public on that specific day. The information may be provided via the Internet, telephone or by someone just showing up unannounced. The FBI receives thousands of complaints each day. Persons who just show up are referred to as walk-ins. Most agents do not like working complaint duty because of the walk-ins. Many times, a walk-in is the type of paranoid person you see on the evening news who, after his fourth Lone Star beer, sees a spaceship fly out of his barn.

I recall one walk-in when I was in my first year with the FBI. This person sat across the table from me in a room secured from the rest of the office. I intuitively knew something was not right with this guy's head. He proceeded in detailing how he was a spy for the Central Intelligence Agency (CIA). He slipped me a note containing letters and numbers which he swore were codes. He wanted me to take the codes to the CIA for him. When I asked him why he could not take the "codes" himself, he said he was being followed and could not go into the CIA's building. When I questioned him about why he could overtly appear at the FBI office when he was being followed, he became silent. Then he became severely red-faced and the room developed a noxious odor. When I realized the walk-in had just defecated in his pants, I promptly and physically escorted him out of the building. I asked a senior agent whether I should write a report on this incident. Without missing a beat, the senior agent responded, "no, just call the CIA and tell them one of their spies just took a dump in our office, and that they should come and get him!" Another senior agent stopped me in the middle of my dialing, "Rick, he's joking!"

A few months later, I was on complaint duty, again. A middle-aged male walked into the office and told me a story of how the government had placed a microchip in his head. The purpose of the microchip was to communicate with aliens from outer space. After a few minutes with this guy, I left the interview room and went to our break room. I returned with a box of foil. I told this guy there had been a rash of people who the government did this to and the foil would help. I proceeded in wrapping his wrist in the foil and told him the microchip would not work if he kept the foil on. I also told him that Martians did not like foil. Finally, I told him that if any aliens reappeared, he should go to the United States Secret Service (USSS) and ask to speak with someone on the "metro alien" task force. I conveniently failed to mention to the walk-in that this task force addressed aliens from various regions of Africa committing Nigerian fraud and identity theft scams.

It is easy to see why agents hated complaint duty, mostly because of the really messed up people in this world. However, as we have seen in recent history, some of the most significant cases are made or missed based on the complaint duty agent's judgment to proceed with a case or dismiss the matter.

On an early morning in May 2012, Skilly was on complaint duty. He encountered a walk-in who wanted to provide information regarding a real estate investment scheme. As violent crime agents are humorously referred to as "knuckle draggers", with T-rex brains, Skilly humbly recognized he needed someone a little bit more familiar with fraud matters. Therefore, I assisted with the interview at his request.

The "walk-in" identified himself as Dr. David Stephens[20]. We subsequently discovered Dr. Stephens was a well-known surgeon in the North Texas area. The matter he was about to discuss was currently in a civil lawsuit. He informed us he had previously appeared at the Dallas office of the FBI about a year earlier to file a complaint; however, the FBI agents in Dallas had shown no interest. He was informed by agents on the Economic Crime squad that the FBI would wait and see how the civil lawsuit played out before initiating a criminal case. Dr. Stephens also filed a complaint with the Securities and Exchange Commission but had heard nothing from them. He could not understand how the FBI would not get involved in this fraudulent matter, so coming to the Frisco office of the FBI was his final desperate plea to get the FBI to initiate a case.

I recalled a story by one of our FBI instructors at the FBI Academy. This instructor told us of a complaint he once took while working in West Virginia. The complaint was made by a mother in her 50s. She was someone who lived in a trailer park and her appearance was not very presentable. She had appeared at the FBI for a second time in a last-ditch effort to get someone to help

---

[20] Fictional name

her locate her teenage daughter. This mother had gone to her local police on several occasions and had complained to the FBI on a previous occasion. She felt something bad had happened to her daughter; however, she had nothing more than a hunch, a mother's intuition. She wanted someone to contact a person named Mitch Swanson[21], who had previously been involved with her daughter. Since Swanson lived in a different jurisdiction, the local police informed the mother they would not get involved and recommended she contact the police in the jurisdiction where Swanson lived, which was in Virginia. The police wrote off the complaint as a runaway situation. In the mother's previous meeting with the FBI, the FBI agent determined that since the police considered the situation was a runaway case, and since the FBI does not get involved in runaways, the FBI did not act on the complaint. The FBI instructor described in detail the mother's heartache and desperation when he met with her.

Our FBI instructor told us that we should always ask ourselves two questions when taking a complaint. The first question is what can I do? The second question is what should I do? The first question deals with the legalities and authorities of our badge. The second question deals with more of a morality issue. It goes beyond the authority of our badge and centers on righteousness. Our instructor contacted the FBI field office in the area of Swanson's residence to obtain a local reference for a good violent crime detective in the police department. The instructor had to convince the detective to contact Swanson despite having no open case and no evidence of wrongdoing. The detective ultimately agreed to go interview Swanson about the missing teenager. After the interview, the detective contacted the instructor

---

[21] Fictional name

40

and informed him that something was not right about Swanson. Within six months, the detective had opened a case, gathered some circumstantial evidence against Swanson, and ultimately obtained a confession from Swanson disclosing he had killed the missing girl. The instructor was present with the mother when her daughter's body was uncovered.

However tragic, the point of the story is to do anything and everything within your power to assist those who have been the victim of a violent or financial crime; and not to pass the buck because some other authority was convinced there was no case.

————————————

Dr. Stephens exhaustively explained how he became the victim of an elaborate real estate investment scheme perpetrated by members of HBLCO. He lost over $1 million dollars based on the misrepresentations made by Lucas Jr. and his Uncle Chip.

In 2008, Dr. Stephens attended an investor presentation at the HBLCO office in Carrollton, Texas at the recommendation of his swimming associate, Mark Emerson. Dr. Stephens told us that Emerson was a collegiate swimmer at Southern Methodist University during the 1980's. Emerson confidentially told Dr. Stephens that an insider at Disney told a family member of his employer (HBLCO) that Disney was acquiring land near Celina, Texas to build a theme park. According to Emerson, the insider information was not known to the general public.

Dr. Stephens cautiously accepted Emerson's invitation and attended the meeting at HBLCO. All the investors were compelled to sign a non-disclosure agreement stating they would not disclose any of the information presented, specifically the fact that Disney was planning a theme park in North Texas. Dr. Stephens described the presentation as a power point presentation that lasted three to four hours. Lucas Jr. was the main person who delivered the presentation. However, Uncle Chip and Emerson also provided information in support of the presentation.

Lucas Jr. initially informed the audience that he had over-heard "someone" who said Disney was going to build an amuse-ment park in North Texas, and that the amusement park would be called Frontier Disney DFW. Dr. Stephens was informed the announcement for the park was scheduled for January 2, 2009. Based on the information, HBLCO started buying land surround-ing the location of the proposed theme park. The mindset was that once the general public got wind of the Disney's intentions, then the land value would increase exponentially.

Lucas Jr. showed the investors an elaborately detailed aerial map of the proposed Frontier Disney. He offered a power point slide that depicted the land located west of the Dallas North Toll-way and east of Farm-to-Market (FM) 1385, between FM428 and FM455. This land straddled Collin County and Denton Coun-ty, both in the Eastern District of Texas. HBLCO representa-tives assured the investors that land values would skyrocket after the announcement of the Disney theme park was made. Then, HBLCO would sell the land to developers for a huge return on their investment.

Lucas Jr. also showed the investors some power point slides of Disney rides, a movie park, condominiums, retail agreements between Disney and high-end retailers, a letter from Southwest Airlines reflecting they would assist with a new airport in the vicin-ity of the park, and a prospectus. Dr. Stephens confirmed that all the documents shown to the investors were elaborate and provid-ed by Lucas Jr.

Uncle Chip and Lucas Jr. presented two avenues for investing. One was to purchase the land outright. The second avenue was to purchase the land-option contracts. The difference in investment methods was whether there would be land that could provide security to the investors. If all else failed, purchased land could be sold to repay investors and help minimize their losses. This would not be so if land option contracts were purchased. This was the same pitch which they had made to Sean Hartman and the other investors.

Lucas Jr. showed the investors the letter dated May 21, 2005, written by Ken Webb, Excalibur Management Group, to Jay Rasulo, which claimed he had purchased sufficient land in Texas for Disney. Lucas Jr. showed Dr. Stephens and other investors the letter dated August 15, 2005, from Mr. Rasulo to the Excalibur Management Team regarding the Disney representative who would be running Frontier Disney. Lucas Jr. also showed the investors architectural drawings of the concept plan for the theme park. Dr. Stephens said the slides were convincing. The investors were not allowed to have copies of any slides or other documents pertaining to the presentation.

Based solely on the representations made by Uncle Chip and Lucas Jr, Dr. Stephens invested $1,050,000 over a three-month period. He invested in the land options for three different joint ventures which involved different acreages of land around the proposed theme park. The joint ventures were the Old 686 JV, the OHOAD JV, and STS Partners JV. The funds passed through the bank account of the HBLCO at First National Bank[22] located within the Northern District of Texas. However, of his total investment, $700,000 went to a title company that banked at Legacy

---

[22] Fictional Name

43

Texas Bank, Plano, Texas. This was significant because it established money coming into the Eastern District of Texas, thereby, providing venue for me to work the case with the prosecutors in the Eastern District of Texas.

The announcement was never made, and Disney never came to Texas. When Dr. Stephens questioned Lucas Jr. regarding the theme park, Lucas Jr. unsympathetically told Dr. Stephens he was not the only investor who lost money. Lucas Jr. offered no further explanation or apology.

Dr. Stephens alleged Lucas Jr. fabricated the entire Disney theme park to make money. Dr. Stephens subsequently did some research on Lucas Jr. and noticed that on Lucas Jr.'s MySpace page was a photo of Lucas Jr. standing next to his red Ferrari. As Dr. Stephens bowed his head and looked over the top of his reading glasses, he deflatingly said, "I fear my money purchased the Ferrari."

Dr. Stephens had been in a civil suit against HBLCO, Lucas Jr., and Uncle Chip for three years. During the lawsuit, Dr. Stephens discovered an email dated November 4, 2007, with a subject line that reflected "Fake Disney". The email contained an attached article referencing that Disney was opening a resort in Texas. The article was verbatim of an article Dr. Stephens had received during the presentation, except his article referenced an actual Disney resort in Hawaii. He insisted this was part of the scam. In an excerpt of the email, Mr. Rasulo stated "Texas has been amongst our most requested Disney Vacation Club getaway locations..."

Also, in a civil deposition related to the lawsuit, a Disney representative who had knowledge of Disney's business development, testified how Disney was not moving to Texas. Dr. Stephens discovered from other investors the letter allegedly written by Mr. Webb to Mr. Rasulo was false. He also discovered from other investors the architectural drawing of the concept plan was a Photoshopped drawing of an actual theme park in Kansas.

After hearing Dr. Stephens' story, I too was confused why the agents in Dallas failed to initiate a case. If Dr. Stephens had been the only victim in this case, it still would have been worth pursuing because of the misrepresentations made and the amount of money he lost. Additionally, investment fraud has a five-year statute of limitations which means law enforcement has five years from the last criminal act to indict a person for fraud. This meant that at most, the FBI had approximately one year to indict the subjects responsible for the fraud. Since Dr. Stephens stated there were numerous victims of Lucas' scheme, there was no telling how high the losses could go.

To ensure we had adequate leads which we could follow up, I requested names of other investors, specifically the names of the investors who discovered the false documents and concept plan. Dr. Stephens informed us that an investor named Darius Garland[23] lost money, and that Mr. Garland was the investor who discovered bogus documents. Per Dr. Stephens, Mr. Garland was a former professional basketball player who lost approximately $3 million dollars. Dr. Stephens also provided an HBLCO document that contained some of the names of investors, the joint venture they were in, and the amount of money they invested.

Skilly and I ensured we asked the relevant questions to address the elements of a federal violation. Investment schemes are usually prosecuted under the mail fraud or wire fraud statutes because they are straightforward and broad statutes. They are similar statutes in

---

[23] Fictional name of professional athlete

that there must be an intent to defraud; there must be a scheme to defraud or a scheme to obtain money or property; and they must involve the use of a mailing by an interstate carrier (for mail fraud) or the use of an interstate wire transmission (for wire fraud). Basically, if the United States Postal Service, Federal Express, or UPS were used to further the scheme, there would be a violation of the mail fraud statute. If investors' funds were wired to Texas from out of state or if fraudulent emails were sent, usually this satisfied the element of a wire crossing state lines for the wire fraud statute. The biggest challenge would be to ensure there were overt acts committed in the Eastern District of Texas. The reason I wanted the overt acts to be in the Eastern District of Texas was because I wanted the USAO in the Eastern District of Texas to prosecute those responsible for this scheme. The USAO in Plano had a good reputation for being aggressive with white-collar criminals, the Assistant United States Attorneys (AUSA) were easy to work with, and their reputation for fairness was beyond reproach. We had wire transfers ending up in a bank located in the Eastern District of Texas, the subject property was in Collin County and Denton County, both counties being in the Eastern District of Texas, and we certainly had enough allegations of fraud.

Also worth mentioning, we had the name of Disney being misused, a professional basketball player being defrauded, and several million dollars in losses. This case certainly had jury appeal. Although I was wrapping up one of the biggest mortgage fraud cases in the country at the time, I requested my supervisor open and assign this case to me. The next step was to get an AUSA on board.

Chapter Nine
"The Commissioner"

When Shamoil Shipchandler started work at the US Attorney's Office in Plano, he was young and ready to hit the ground running. Shamoil completed his undergraduate studies at Middlebury College, one of the 'little ivy's', and obtained his law degree from Cornell Law School. He was by far one of the most competent and enthusiastic prosecutors I had worked with in 25 years. Working with Shamoil was one of the top reasons that made my job fun. Shamoil was bright, funny, and a trusted friend. When other agents in the FBI or other agencies asked my opinion about Shamoil, I would always say the same thing, "He's a good friend and the only prosecutor who knows the case better than the case agent." Shamoil loved a good legal argument and was not opposed to going to trial unlike most AUSAs in other judicial districts where I would have to take a case once in every blue moon. Like all AUSAs, he would prefer that a defendant plead guilty, but he also loved making an argument to a jury in front of a United States District Judge. He was a gladiator of the law and the courtroom was his Coliseum. There is an old saying that deals with the partnership between FBI agents and AUSAs: experienced agents teach young AUSAs how to be prosecutors and experienced AUSAs teach young agents how to be investigators. This was certainly true with Shamoil and me; however, by the time Shamoil left the USAO, he had become the teacher.

Shamoil and I worked a lot of cases together, and several of those cases went to trial. Since trial preparation involves extensive man hours, the relationship between the agent and the prosecutor must be good. The agent, if he/she is doing his/her job, must be flexible. It is imperative the agent is available to work evenings, weekends and holidays, if necessary, because you can bet the prosecutor is working the same hours. You either become close or you become miserable.

I have known agents and supervisors who complained about requests made by prosecutors during trial preparation. I once took a conference call from an FBI supervisor and two agents from the Northern District of Texas (Dallas). The supervisor wanted my input on "how to get along" with a particular prosecutor in the Eastern District of Texas. What the FBI supervisor did not know was that the prosecutor had previously expressed his dissatisfaction to me about the work ethic of the case agent. Apparently, the case agent refused to get what the prosecutor needed and refused to work after 5:00 pm. My response to the supervisor was simple and blunt, "Have your agents do what the prosecutor needs them to do because the prosecutor is busy filing motions, responding to motions, writing a pre-trial brief and everything else behind the scenes," and, "Try to work when the prosecutor is working". I questioned the integrity of any agent who is off enjoying their weekend while the prosecutor is stuck in an office preparing for trial. Finally, I told the supervisor to prohibit his agents with bad attitudes from working cases in the Eastern District of Texas because they were going to destroy the relationship we had established with the prosecutors. The supervisor thanked me, but I believe he was surprised I responded to him in such a direct manner.

Shamoil and I had fun experiences with the trials we had. We were once prosecuting a defendant in an investment fraud scheme.

As part of the trial, we had to put victims on the stand who would appeal to the emotions of the jurors. One of the victims we chose was a six-foot, four-inch gentleman who weighed near 400 pounds. His name was Jim Nelson[24]. Mr. Nelson had lost his life savings, which was only a couple thousand dollars, in the investment scam. We flew Mr. Nelson in from Seattle, Washington where he used to be deep-sea fisherman. Mr. Nelson had flown into Sherman, Texas the night before his testimony so I did not get to see him until the next morning. When I met Mr. Nelson for breakfast to secure his ride to the courthouse, he told me he had an issue with his wardrobe. In federal courthouses, males are required to wear a tie and a jacket, so I instructed Mr. Nelson to bring a shirt, tie and jacket. On the morning Mr. Nelson was to testify, he came down from his room wearing an old polo shirt with an old mustard stain on the chest. I could hear the embarrassment in his voice when he informed me the shirt and jacket he brought had not been worn in 15 years, when he was 200 pounds lighter. I looked at Mr. Nelson and smiled because I recalled what it was like growing up with little money in Austin, Texas. I asked Mr. Nelson if he brought a tie. He responded, "yes but I don't know how to tie it". I placed the tie under his polo collar and tied him a half-Windsor knot. It was obvious the tie had not been worn in a while too. The tie came down half-way to Mr. Nelson's naval. I purposely extended the back part of the tie so it would be longer than the front, fatter part of the tie. His testimony regarding his loss of money and his appearance would be extremely appealing to the jury.

Mr. Nelson was called to the stand after the elderly woman who was on an oxygen tank had completed her testimony. We had to ask for the judge's permission to escort Mr. Nelson to the witness

---

[24] Fictional name

stand because he had trouble walking due to an injury suffered in a fishing-boat accident and because of his weight. The judge granted the request for me to walk behind Mr. Nelson until he got on the stand. This was to break Mr. Nelson's fall should he collapse. As we were walking by the defense table, I overheard the defense investigator comment to the defense attorney in a loud whisper, "This is an f***ing nightmare" causing me to openly chuckle.

At the conclusion of the trial, Shamoil and I had to escort Mr. Nelson to his transportation so he could go back to the Dallas-Fort Worth airport. Because of Mr. Nelson's weight, he had an overwhelmingly difficult time getting into the back seat of the sedan, simply because he did not fit. In fact, Mr. Nelson got half of his posterior onto the back seat and then he began to tip over towards the curb of the street. I instantly put my hands on Mr. Nelson's side to keep him from falling out of the car. Using the curb for leverage, I exhaustingly pushed Mr. Nelson into the car and barely got the door to close. When I stood up, Shamoil looked at the sweat dripping from my forehead and laughed. To this day, Shamoil still tells the story of "other collateral duties" agents endure.

One of the many other duties of FBI agents is to conduct interviews for foreign law enforcement agencies under MLAT agreements. MLAT stands for Mutual Legal Assistance Treaty. This assistance was rare in the Frisco RA. However, on one occasion, I conducted an interview for a law enforcement agency in South America. Before sending the results of the interview back to South America, the USAO had to sign off on a letter. This duty fell upon Shamoil, as the supervising attorney-in-charge. When Shamoil signed the letter, he placed an interesting title under his name; "Commissioner". The agents in the squad area had a good chuckle about this title because prosecutors were simply referred to as AUSAs. It was a cool title and Shamoil jokingly became known as the Commissioner from that point on.

After the interview of Dr. Stephens, I called Shamoil to inform him about the allegations and to get a prosecutive opinion on the matter. Before a full investigation is conducted into any complaint, it is FBI protocol to ensure the USAO will prosecute any and all subjects of a case if a federal violation can be proven. This communication establishes two things: one, it ensures the FBI does not waste its time (and tax dollars) if the USAO does not believe a federal crime has been committed, and two, it ensures the case is prosecuted in the correct federal judicial district. If the USAO declines to prosecute the subjects for one of a handful of reasons, then the information is provided to local law enforcement. If the USAO agrees to the prosecute the subjects, then a full investigation is initiated, which may include conducting further interviews, serving subpoenas for records, serving subpoenas to have witnesses testify in front of Federal Grand Juries, consensually recording various conversations, conducting searches and possibly surveilling the subject. Basically, the FBI will use any and all means, within the law, to determine whether the allegations of a crime are true or untrue. During the phone call to obtain the prosecutive opinion, an AUSA will be assigned to the case.

Shamoil agreed that a fraud had occurred and that this new matter warranted a full investigation. The investigation appeared to have a large amount of losses for numerous investors. We both knew that investment/securities fraud cases usually fell into two categories: one is the misrepresentation of material facts by the subject(s) so they can get investors to part with their funds; and two, the misuse of investors' funds, usually for lavish lifestyles of the subject(s) which would usually be uncovered by tracing the funds. The second type of scheme sometimes involves a situation referred to as a Ponzi scheme. Ponzi schemes are standard with conmen. A Ponzi scheme is where a conman will solicit investors to invest in some type of project, investment, or scheme with the promise of high rates of returns. The conman will misuse the investors' funds to pay for his lavish lifestyle. The conman will continue to solicit investors into his scheme, and he will use new investors' funds to pay the initial investors, thereby creating the appearance of a false return on investment. This can go on for years as in the case of Bernie Madoff. The last investors to be sucked into a Ponzi scheme are the ultimate victims.

Shamoil asked the anticipated question, "Were there uses of mailings or interstate wires in furtherance of the scheme that occurred in the Eastern District of Texas". I responded that the location of the overt acts had not been established, yet. However, the property in question was located entirely within the Eastern District of Texas. I jokingly informed Shamoil that if I could not establish the venue was in the Eastern District of Texas, then I was not the extraordinary agent I thought I was. Shamoil agreed to open a case and at my request, to be the prosecutor should the FBI prove the allegations of fraud.

Chapter Ten
"Lying, Stealing and Cheating"

Fraud consists of activities conducted in an unethical or illegal manner by one or more people. The unethical or illegal activities are designed to give an advantage, usually financial, to the perpetrating party. In my own terms, if someone must lie, steal, or cheat to make a buck, then that person is doing something unethical. If the unethical activity involves the use of an interstate mail carrier, an interstate communication, or a computer, then there is a particularly good chance the person is violating a federal statute.

Federal Grand Jury subpoenas were immediately requested from Shamoil to serve on the entities we knew about. White-collar cases are known as paper cases and as cliché as it may be, you usually follow the money to resolve the case. We knew where HBLCO was conducting its banking so we subpoenaed all records related to HBLCO. Obtaining the bank records accomplished several things. The bank records showed us the source of deposited funds. The source of deposits was huge because this identified the names of investors/victims and possible addresses for investors (now we knew who and where to contact witnesses). The bank records showed us the method of deposited items such as check versus wire transfer. Checks must be mailed; hence, we had mail fraud and wires possibly crossed state lines; hence, we had wire fraud. The bank records also showed us the location from which the funds originated. All of this was necessary to prove the elements of wire fraud or mail fraud. The use of funds might show us intent, especially if the funds were misapplied; they showed us which properties were purchased which would be necessary to tell a Federal Grand Jury if we got to the point of indictment; and they gave us a date for which to measure the statute of limitations. Remember, we only had five years to prove a wire fraud or mail fraud case, which was generally measured from the date of transaction. By the time Dr. Stephens filed his complaint with the FBI in Frisco, we were already three and one-half years into the statute of limitations. Therefore, we had approximately 18 months from the last overt act. This also meant we were losing fraudulent counts, daily.

One of the many things I learned as a new agent was to always investigate and prepare a case like you were going to trial. This ensured all your ducks were in a row. An FBI agent needed to anticipate any and all questions from an FBI supervisor, the Assistant US Attorney, the defense attorney, and the United States District Judge. It is okay to tell someone you do not know something but if you say it too many times then you just look incompetent. An FBI agent never wanted to take a half-baked case to a prosecutor. I would like to believe my practices were why Shamoil and the other AUSAs at the US Attorney's Office had confidence in prosecuting the defendants in the cases I took to them.

When I finally received the subpoenaed bank records, I realized the number of investors involved with this case were more than anticipated. There were over 250 investors. The amount of money flowing through the bank account was in the millions. The case instantly had more jury appeal.

I learned in an interview with Sean Hartman, the Dallas attorney who invested in the initial land deal in 2006, that he had filed his own lawsuit against HBLCO and its principals. This lawsuit was vital to the investigation by the FBI because it gave us access to volumes of documents provided by Lucas Jr. One of the problems with white-collar cases is by the time the case gets to the FBI, the records are stale and may have been destroyed. Civil suits usually acquire records prior to criminal investigations. As such, records are preserved in the form of civil exhibits. The civil suit also provided us with the three depositions taken of Lucas Jr.

Obviously, Dr. Stephens had a good story to tell. However, his information was just allegations until the facts could be confirmed. This would be done through the review of voluminous documents and extensive interviews of the witnesses. I needed another convincing investor who was victimized by the representatives at HBLCO. Someone who would provide a dominating presence at trial, should Lucas Jr. not plead guilty.

Chapter Eleven
"In for a Penny, in for a Pound"

I remember watching Darius Garland[25] play basketball at SMU back in the early 1980s when SMU was still part of the Southwest Conference. He was an imposing player who averaged 15 rebounds and 20 points per game. Mr. Garland was a consensus All-American, a team that included some of the great players in college and ultimately the National Basketball Association (NBA). He was drafted in the first round of the NBA draft. Over his eleven-year career in the pros, he was considered one of the best utility players in the NBA. Owing to Mr. Garland's collegiate career at SMU, which is located in the heart of Dallas, Texas, Mr. Garland was considered a local sports celebrity around the Dallas area. Mr. Garland retired in his birth state of Georgia, where I located him.

In the fall of 2012, I called Mr. Garland to request an interview. Mr. Garland was eager to sit down with me and share his story. He said he was surprised and encouraged that the FBI was finally looking into the activities of the HBLCO. You see, Mr. Garland had also complained to the FBI in Dallas approximately 18 months earlier. He was told by the agent to sue HBLCO. Mr. Garland considered suing HBLCO but decided against it because he no longer had the disposable funds to pay an attorney.

---

[25] Fictional name and stats of a professional athlete

Mr. Garland agreed to the interview, so I flew to Atlanta, Georgia the next week. Mr. Garland's interview was conducted at the FBI Atlanta Field Office. He was a towering person and I think he surprised several of the employees at the office when he entered. The employees were obvious fans. Some took photographs with him and others kept passing by the interview room to get a glimpse of him.

After some small talk, Mr. Garland detailed his association with representatives of the HBLCO. In early January 2007, he had received a call from Mark Emerson, an old acquaintance of his. As previously stated, Mr. Garland and Emerson were both scholar athletes at SMU in the 1980s. Emerson had informed Mr. Garland that he (Emerson) was working at a real estate company called HBLCO. Emerson told Mr. Garland that representatives of HBLCO had come into some confidential information that Disney intended to build a theme park in North Texas. Emerson then told him that when word got out about the theme park, the value of the land surrounding the theme park would go through the roof. In anticipation of the announcement of the theme park, HBLCO was buying up all the land they could. Emerson further said that the announcement would be made on February 4, 2007, during the Super Bowl. Mr. Garland had been told that Lucas Jr. had an inside source at Disney and the source was giving HBLCO detailed information. Emerson thus offered his old friend, who had money, the opportunity to make more money on inside information.

Mr. Garland had been so intrigued by what Emerson was telling him that he did not do any due diligence on his own. He wholly relied on the information provided by Emerson (which came from Lucas Jr.) In January 2007, Mr. Garland wired approximately $600,000 to the HBLCO bank account at First National Bank for the purchase of an interest in the Celina 209 Joint

Venture. Mr. Garland thus had pooled his money with others for the purchase of actual land in this joint venture.

The Super Bowl came and went without the announcement from Disney. When Mr. Garland questioned Emerson, Emerson told him to be patient, and that Disney would make the announcement at a later date. He had been shown the 2005 letters between the Excalibur Management Group and Disney. He had also been shown the conceptual plan of the park. Based on the assurances made by Emerson and Lucas Jr., Mr. Garland proceeded to invest more money.

Owing to the investors' concerns over the "canceled" announcement during Super Bowl 2007, Lucas Jr. had naturally known he needed to provide more information about Frontier Disney.

In March 2007, he provided a photo to Uncle Chip for the purpose of showing the investors. The photo was of Jay Rasulo allegedly standing on the stage at the Majestic Theatre in Dallas, Texas. The Majestic Theatre is a nostalgic structure built in 1921, and it is all that remains of the once thriving Theatre Row in Dallas. Lucas, Jr. told Uncle Chip that Mr. Rasulo was rehearsing the speech for the Frontier Disney announcement. Above Mr. Rasulo was a big-screen video showing Mickey Mouse hovering over Cinderella's castle and the words "Disney Frontier DFW". Lucas, Jr. encouraged his Uncle Chip to show the photo to the investors but cautioned Uncle Chip about allowing them to keep a copy of the photo. Lucas Jr. knew the photo would provide relief and reassurance to the investors. Upon seeing this photo and hearing the announcement was near, Mr. Garland then invested $100,000 in the Old 686 Joint Venture, $100,000 in Dynavest Joint Venture, and $100,000 in the OHOAD Joint Venture. He recalled the employees at HBLCO said OHOAD was an acronym for One Hell of a Deal. All three of these investments had been for the land option contracts. Hence, there would have been no land changing hands until the investors had exercised their option to purchase the land.

Mr. Garland said things started getting out of hand. He admits he had maybe been a bit greedy because he was trying to capitalize on this opportunity. Between April 2007 and August 2007, Mr. Garland had invested several hundred-thousand dollars more. One of Mr. Garland's investments had been in the Crooked Cross property. The name came from the outlining boundaries of the land appearing to resemble a crooked cross when seen on an aerial map.

Lucas Jr. had informed the investors that based on information from his Disney source, the new announcement date would be during the 2008 Super Bowl. The announcement never happened.

Mr. Garland had a lot of money invested into the land deals, so he wanted frequent updates of the progress. He flew to Dallas, Texas to attend one of several presentations he would eventually appear at. This was the first time he met Uncle Chip and Lucas Jr. According to Mr. Garland, Lucas Jr. was obviously in charge of the investor presentations. He showed the investors some power point slides of a map of the park, and informed the investors that Disney was secretly buying land. Lucas Jr. referenced the airport that would be built near the theme park. According to Lucas Jr., the airport would be a hub for Southwest Airlines who was in negotiations to partner with Disney. A shuttle service would be provided to the theme park for the tourists. Everything Lucas Jr. said just made Mr. Garland more comfortable with his investments.

At his first presentation, Mr. Garland signed a non-disclosure agreement. My experience with such agreements is that they are commonly used in business. I have never worked an investor fraud scheme where the investors were not required to sign such an agreement. I have even seen non-disclosure agreements in other securities fraud cases in which it was specifically stated the investors would not discuss information with law enforcement. In the world of white-collar cases, this is what we referred to as a clue. At this presentation, Lucas Jr. showed Mr. Garland and the other investors a document titled Frontier Disney DFW. This document showed how Disney had acquired 15,000 acres of land for the purpose of building its theme park in North Texas.

Since the Disney announcements were never made, the options on the contracts to purchase land would always near the contract expiration date. In order to extend the contracts, more money would be needed from the investors to pay the landowners and keep the contracts valid. Mr. Garland had to borrow an additional half a million dollars to continue paying on the option contract extensions. His rationale was "in for a penny, in for a pound". He explained that he had had so much money invested in this Disney deal that if he had not continued to pay to extend the contracts, then he would have lost everything, which eventually happened. I have seen many victims with this same rationale in my career. At some point, the victim is no longer investing; but instead, is gambling.

By continuing to throw money at the Disney deal, Mr. Garland eventually wired $5,000 to a title company located in McKinney, Texas, which was in the Eastern District of Texas. The wired funds came from a bank outside of the state of Texas. This was the interstate wire and overt act needed to prosecute the subjects of this case in the Eastern District of Texas.

Mr. Garland believed that by the end of the 2008, the real estate market was in a downturn. The value of land was dropping. This concerned him enough that he wanted more frequent updates on the Disney announcement. Each time the announcement was delayed in 2008, the reason would be blamed on the economy.

In 2009, Mr. Garland and another investor named Nicky Stone attended another investor presentation conducted by Lucas Jr. and the others. Both were concerned about the delayed Disney announcements and started to question each other whether the excuses they were given made any sense. There was a break during the presentation where Lucas Jr. went outside to smoke a cigarette. During the break, Mr. Stone seized the opportunity to take some cell phone photos of some of the slides Lucas Jr. had been showing the investors at these presentations. The photos taken included the preliminary concept plan of Frontier Disney which was designed by Law Kingdon Inc.; the letter dated May 21, 2005, from Ken Webb, vice president, EMG to Jay Rasulo, Chairman of Disney Parks and Resorts; a photo of Mr. Rasulo rehearsing the Disney announcement at the Majestic Theatre in Dallas, Texas which included the Frontier Disney logo; and the letter dated August 15, 2005, from Mr. Rasulo to the EMG team making certain representations about the land acquired. These four slides had been presented to all investors at the presentations and Lucas Jr. had insisted that they were given to him by his source at Disney.

Because the photos of the slides were quickly taken by Mr. Stone with his cell phone, they were all a bit blurry. Remember, the investors were prohibited from keeping any of the documents from the presentations. Owing to Mr. Garland and Mr. Stone's, and some other investors' suspicions, Mr. Garland and Mr. Stone started conducting something of their own investigation. What they discovered was alarming.

Mr. Garland and Mr. Stone meticulously transcribed the blurred photos of the 2005 letters. The transcription for the letter dated May 21, 2005 read as follows:

(EMG Logo)
EXCALIBUR MANAGEMENT GROUP

Jay Rasulo
RE: New entrance
5/21/2005

Jay,

Just wanted to updated (*update*) you on the King Ranch Project. We are now at 98% with our land requirements. There are however a few tracks (*tracts*) needed. We still feel that the entrance would be best at the corner of the Dallas North Tollway Expansion and FM428, but a few sellers are not reasonable at this time with selling. So we prepose (*propose*) to move the entrance to FM428 and the DentonCollin (Denton-Collin) County lines. This would almost seal the deal with only one or two tracks (*tracts*) left to purchase, and would be more economical for park plans B, C, and D. As you know both Garrett, Owens, and myself (*I*) will be flying to Hong Kong this Friday to help out (*help*) with some finishing touches on the park and look forward to seeing you. Best wishes on the birth of your new daughter.

/signature/
Ken Webb
Vice President

———————————————

The transcription for the letter dated August 15, 2005 read as follows:

(*Photo of Mickey Mouse*)	Office of Parks & Resorts
Walt Disney Parks and Resorts	500 S. Buena Vista St.
	Burbank, Ca 91501 (*91521*)
	818.560.1000
Excalibur Management Team:	08.15.05

There's a new member joining our team and I thought I would send a little heads up letter. Karl Hotz (*Holtz*) is going to be president of Disney Dallas Ft. Worth. Karl is currently president of Walt Disney World Resort Paris and has been for the past few years. He somehow pulled a rabbit out of a hat by turning this park around and we figured he's just the man for the new market. So please label him as your new problem solver. If you could catch him up on key issues like the roadways, and temperature, or anything else that may be in our "concern folder." Karl is currently on vacation and will be in Burbank sometime next week. It is at that time I will surprise him with his new role at Walt Disney Parks. So if you could set up a care package that I could give him at that time I would be grateful.

Also, you had mentioned previously that certain land tracks (*tracts*) were hard to obtain. Please do what ever (*whatever*) is in your power, to acquire our key tracks (*tracts*) of land. Consider it as a blank check. In conversation with George, I told him not to pay above our redline agreement for the remaining parcels, but I have since changed my mind. It's now crunch time in making our land goal, especially with our upcoming meeting in November on our park layout. I have complete faith in you guys.

Until our next meeting,

/signature/
Jay Rasulo
President Walt Disney Parks & Resorts
500 S. Buena Vista Street
Burbank, Ca 91501 (*91521*)

———————————————

I learned early in my career that an investigator should never take a witness testimony at face value. The investigator should independently confirm all information received from witnesses. As such, I sat down with the blurred letters and transcribed the letters for myself. For several hours, I painstakingly deciphered the letters and wrote what I perceived to be the words in the letters. The result was the same transcription as that of Mr. Garland and Mr. Stone.

Mr. Garland stated by entering certain key words on his Internet search, he found a theme park in Kansas called Wild West World that made his stomach turn. The photo of the preliminary concept plan for Frontier Disney DFW was exactly the same as the photo for the preliminary concept plan for the Wild West World near Wichita, Kansas. Each preliminary concept plan included photos of the people on the main strip and a covered wagon in the background. The logo of the architect firm, Law Kingdon, Inc. was even the same. The only difference was the name of the park and the theme park's logo on the concept pan.

Mr. Garland searched the photo of Jay Rasulo allegedly rehearsing the announcement speech at the Majestic Theatre. The photo showed Mr. Rasulo in a suit on an open stage with a big electronic board in the background that reflected Disney Frontier DFW. The results of his search revealed the exact same photo of Mr. Rasulo making a presentation at Disney's 50th anniversary in New York City. The only difference between the two photos were the Disney logos. Mr. Garland was livid with Lucas Jr. and the rest of the guys at HBLCO. He instantly knew the photos presented to them at the investor presentations were Photoshopped and fraudulent.

In March 2009, Mr. Stone went to the HBLCO office and confronted Lucas Jr. and Uncle Chip while Mr. Garland listened on the cell phone. Lucas Jr. stood behind everything that he represented and affirmed that the photos were real. Mr. Garland and Mr. Stone demanded their money back and followed up with demand letters. They got no response from anyone at HBLCO.

Mr. Garland estimated he lost between $2.5 million and $3 million because of the fraud. Despite this, Mr. Garland wrote off the loss and moved on. I thought he was sort of unemotional about his loss during the interview. Although, his physical presence would command attention in the courtroom, I was a bit disappointed and somewhat surprised he was not a little more irate about the whole situation. Maybe he was simply better at controlling his emotions than I thought I would be if I lost millions of dollars to a conman, or maybe he was just beat down by the whole incident. Prior to trial, Mr. Garland explained his unemotional behavior was due to his repeated complaints to law enforcement and their inaction.

Mr. Garland believed Mark Emerson did not know anything about the fraud. Emerson was just passing on information that Lucas Jr. had provided everyone at HBLCO. Emerson resigned the day after Mr. Garland and Mr. Stone confronted HBLCO about the fraud.

Mr. Garland had no idea some of his invested funds were being used to pay Lucas Jr. a referral fee. He realized some of his money would be used for commissions to the real estate agents, but this would only be on closed deals. This meant no commissions should have been paid on the option contracts because the deals were never closed (land was never purchased). Mr. Garland admitted that if he had known about Lucas Jr.'s receipt of referral fees, this would have been an initial concern of his. Mr. Garland knew there was some risk involved with his investments and he admitted, to some extent, that he had been greedy. However, Mr. Garland asserted it would have been ludicrous to believe a risk of fraud should have been assumed. The fraud made this more than just an investment loss. He confirmed that had he known fraud was part of the presentations or part of the deal, he would never have invested. This is relevant because it showed Mr. Garland, and eventually others I would interview, relied on the information presented to them. This made the misrepresentations material and significant. It showed an obvious intent to defraud the investors.

After reviewing the two letters and the Photoshopped pictures of Mr. Rasulo's speech rehearsal and the preliminary concept plan, I had no doubt fraud was perpetrated. My opinion of the letters was that no Disney executive or any executive would use such ridiculous verbiage and poor grammar in a letter. Also, what kind of real estate employee or Disney executive could not spell the word 'tract'? It was apparent to me the two letters were written by the same person since the word "tract" was misspelled in both letters. The use of phrases such as "seal the deal" and "pulled a rabbit out of a hat" are generally not phrases used by executives in official communications. Finally, I questioned what kind of executive would tell an outside third party the identity of the employee to be named president of a theme park before actually informing the employee.

I thought the use of "King Ranch" in the May letter was sort of revealing. The King Ranch is one of the biggest ranches in Texas, if not the biggest. Most Texans know about the King Ranch. However, the King Ranch is less known outside the State of Texas, especially in places as far away as California. My hunch, a Texan came up with this name, and thus, the letter.

The challenge would be to determine whether only Lucas Jr. was involved or were there others at HBLCO involved as well? What about the alleged Disney source? Was there involvement of a Disney insider?

Chapter Twelve
"It's not Much but it's all I had"

HBLCO collected its initial $7 million related to the Disney theme park in 2006. An additional $53 million from investors passed through the HBLCO bank accounts between 2007 and 2009. According to Mark Emerson, the following entities or property descriptions were created or referenced by HBLCO in order to purchase land or land option contracts surrounding the rumored Disney theme park:

Entity	Acreage
NCJI, LLC	105.089
Celina Land Investments	24.5
Locus Proximus	5.5
Terrae Habendae, Ltd.	94.01
Celina Investments, LP	74.6
Lucas Celina 209	209.54
Old 686 Joint Venture*	686
OHOAD Joint Venture*	83.001
TSIG Land Partners*	24
STS Land Partners*	398.42
Affordable Housing/Major Players*	127
Dynavest*	3228
J Squared*	25

Crooked Cross*   1061
Lambert Property*   10
Dale Hill Property*   9.18

* Denotes option contracts

Numerous investors were interviewed. It was determined from these interviews that between 2007 and 2008, the majority of funds were invested leading up to Frontier Disney DFW announcement dates.

HBLCO took in millions of dollars based on the representation by Lucas Jr. that the Disney announcement would be made at the end of the 2007 Super Bowl, which was inconsistent with witnesses' testimony that the announcement would be made at halftime. Lucas Jr. had said that Disney would have a series of commercials leading up to a live announcement at the end of the game. The winning quarterback would be asked what he was going to do when he left the field. The response by the quarterback would be "I'm going to Frontier Disney DFW." The investors had been shown the 2005 letters between Disney and Excalibur Management Group. They had been informed about how secret land purchases were part of Disney World in Orlando, Florida. They had been told of the land value inflation after the announcement. They were excited to turn over their money in anticipation of the Super Bowl announcement and the guaranty that their return on investment would be ten-fold.

Of course, on Super Bowl Sunday, February 4, 2007, there had been no announcement, and Lucas Jr. had made his excuse about Disney having problems with the land acquisition, hence postponing the announcement until the next year's Super Bowl event.

Naturally, the investors were unhappy about Lucas Jr.'s excuse for the delay and he had to come up with something to allay their misgivings. Hence the now infamous 'photo' of Jay Rasulo at the Majestic Theatre in Dallas, Texas which made the investors relax again.

Investors nevertheless continued to ask for updates from Lucas Jr.'s source about Frontier Disney. The primary reason was because many of the investors had invested in the option contracts. When the option contracts were about to expire, the investors would be called upon to pay more money to extend the contract. This needed to be done throughout 2007 since the new proposed announcement date was not scheduled until the 2008 Super Bowl. One of the documents Lucas, Jr. produced and showed to investors was a prospectus showing different phases of Frontier Disney. The prospectus discussed six theme parks, a lake and a tram system. Phase 1 included condos, high-end retail shops, Frontierland, PGA golf courses, a water park, and an airport. Phase 2 through phase 4 included a Texas version of Epcot Center called Texcot, a TV/movie studio complex, a sports complex, and an animal park.

As extended option contracts were about to expire, Lucas Jr. continued to provide information from his alleged source to ease the investors' minds about paying more money. In an email dated August 18, 2007, Lucas Jr. reported to Uncle Chip that Kendall Kent[26], a local news anchor, had attended a meeting where the Disney announcement was discussed. Ms. Kent, who was a high-school friend of Lucas Jr., was an attractive and very reputable news anchor in Dallas. Her name alone, added credence to the Frontier Disney story. According to Lucas Jr., she confirmed that

---

[26] Fictional name

70

Disney was coming to Texas. Uncle Chip then dutifully provided this information to the investors.

On February 3, 2008, Super Bowl Sunday had arrived. The New York Giants upset the undefeated New England Patriots 17-14. This game was remembered for Plaxico Burress' "helmet catch." Needless to say, the Disney announcement for Frontier Disney was not made. As expected, the investors renewed their concerns. Lucas Jr., Uncle Chip and the rest of the HBLCO sales-persons were bombarded with questions. Lucas Jr. said his Disney source rescheduled the announcement for July 4th (Friday) and that he (Lucas, Jr.) would be getting more details soon. To ease the tensions of the investors, Lucas Jr. concocted more documents, claiming he had received them from his source. He gave them the Final Concept Plan which included:

Texcot (Texas' version of Epcot);

Rides at Frontier Disney which included such rides as 'Space Mountain—Houston We Have a Problem'; 'Texas Thunder Mountain Railroad'; 'Frontier Wild West'; and 'Davy Crockett's Shooting Arcade';

Shops at Frontier Disney which included Neiman Marcus; Gucci; Louis Vuitton; Ralph Lauren; and Dolce & Gabbana to name a few; and

Texas Animal Frontier.

This reassured the investors, again, and again, they eagerly paid money to extend the option contracts. However, July 4th came and went without an announcement.

However, investors were now vigorously questioning wheth-er Frontier Disney was real. Investor Nicky Stone warned Uncle

Chip and Lucas, Jr., "If this project is not legitimate, I will burn your asses." Mr. Stone was very flamboyant with his terminology.

"It's real, I promise", responded Lucas Jr., going on to advise that, "My source said the new announcement for Frontier Disney would occur during the Beijing Olympic Games." These were scheduled between August 8, 2008 and August 24, 2008. Lucas Jr. was able to extend his deceit, but he realized he had to conjure up more documents, which he did, managing to maintain the appearance that Frontier Disney was legitimate and quieting the investors yet again. He even provided the plans for the "1215 Luxury Hotel Rooms" for the Grand Texan Adventure Hotel. (The "1215 Luxury Hotel Rooms" will prove relevant, later.) The plans included exterior designs, a huge lake, the lobby, and aerial photos of the designs. More money was invested based on these plans.

By the end of the Olympic Games, no announcement for Frontier Disney had been made—of course. However, Lucas, Jr. was prepared for the investors' uproar. On August 22, 2008, he produced a memorandum he allegedly received from his contact. The letter was ostensibly from Bob Iger, CEO of Disney. The memorandum briefly discussed the opening of Frontier Disney. Along with the memorandum, Lucas Jr. provided advertisement photos. A sample of the advertisement photos included the following:

> Mickey Mouse and Minnie Mouse in cowboy gear standing on a Texas highway beside a sign reflecting a Texas flag. The phrase above the flag read "Welcome to Texas." The phrase below the flag read "Frontier Disney DFW." Printed on the blue sky in the background was the Disney Parks logo and the phrase, "Mickey & The Gang Arrive in the Lone Star State Summer 2011!"

The Dallas skyline with an emphasis on Reunion Tower. Reunion Tower is a conspicuous structure in downtown Dallas. It is a tall silo-shaped structure with a glass sphere at the top. The advertisement had been Photoshopped to include two smaller spheres on top of the larger sphere to create the appearance of mouse ears. Printed on the blue sky in the background was the phrase, "A Magical Mouse Comes to Big D, Summer 2011!"

A satellite photo shot of the earth. In California, Florida, Texas, Hong Kong and Paris a Cinderella castle was at each location. Printed on the night sky in the background was the phrase, "Introducing Frontier Disney Dallas Ft. Worth, The First of Three New Disney Parks Worldwide! The Magic Arrives in North Texas Early Summer 2011."

These advertisements and others were outlandishly creative and convincing as far as the investors were concerned. They facilitated the receipt of even more money from investors, especially right before the next announcement date scheduled for October 1, 2008.

On September 29, 2008, the Dow Jones Industrial Average fell more than 770 points or 7 percent. Lucas Jr. advised that his source stated the market crash delayed the October announcement until November 1, 2008. More time meant more money would be invested in the land option contracts.

In October 2008, the Dow Jones Industrial Average continued its historic decline. Lucas Jr. declared the market crash would delay the November announcement but assured the investors the announcement would be made. Investors continued to place new money in the deals and extended their option contracts, although, their eagerness had faded. There was now a reluctance. However, as Darius Garland put it, "in for a penny, in for a pound."

On Friday, November 14, 2008, Lucas Jr. informed the investors, through an email to Uncle Chip, that Disney executives had gathered in the Crescent Hotel in Dallas to prepare for the announcement. However, during the meeting, Jay Rasulo was notified his wife and young daughter had been in a serious car accident. As such, Mr. Rasulo had to rush back to California. Lucas Jr. said the November announcement date would be delayed until the following Monday. Owing to their concern for the legitimacy of Frontier Disney, investors Mr. Garland and Mr. Stone contacted the hospital in Los Angeles where Mr. Rasulo's daughter was supposedly taken. When they called Mt. Sinai Hospital, they asked for Ms. Rasulo's room and they were transferred. Since the transferred phone call was enough confirmation for them, they hung up. What they did not realize was the hospital operator was transferring them to the admittance operator.

Ultimately, Lucas Jr. informed Uncle Chip that according to his Disney source, Disney would permanently delay the announcement due to the US economy doing so poorly. The investors were not only devastated, but they were also incensed. Their anger with Lucas Jr. and Uncle Chip was uncontrollable.

One investor, Wilfred Waters[27], had invested $80,000 in the option contracts. Of this money, $40,000 came from liquidated savings bonds which was supposed to be used for his retirement. During his interview, Waters tearfully informed me, "It's not much but it's all I had."

---

[27] Fictional name

Chapter Thirteen
"Not Insider Trading"

As subpoenaed documents began rolling in, I confirmed my belief after the Dr. Stephens' interview that this was not just an ordinary investment scheme. I would go on to comb through thousands of documents including bank records, title records, maps, zoning records, depositions and exhibits, investor records, public records, etc. I would also interview numerous investors and witnesses.

Sometimes an agent is assigned a case where it is hard to feel sorry for the victim of a crime simply, because the victim is a poor excuse of a human being. I once had a bankruptcy case where the defendant in the case was charged with physically assaulting one of the creditors. Basically, the defendant punched the creditor a couple of times on the courthouse steps. After interviewing the creditor, I reported to the Assistant US Attorney assigned to the case that the creditor, who was such a vile person, deserved what he got. Meeting the victims in this case confirmed to me that the actions of Lucas Jr. were most definitely worth investigating. I talked to victims who had lost their life savings, victims who lost the money they had put away for their children's college education, victims who had to return to the workforce because their retirement money was gone. Some might argue that if you cannot afford to lose money, you should not be investing in speculative projects, such as Frontier Disney. However, the risk of any real-estate investment should be whether the project comes to fruition, not will the promoter of the project be defrauding me and stealing my money.

During trial, some blogs and one of the local newspapers inappropriately opined that the victims deserved what they got by trying to profit on insider information. There are arguments for and against what the investors were doing. My rationale was there was a huge difference between self-interest and selfishness or greed. I do not believe the investors were trying to control the markets or competitors or the sellers. I believe they were 'acting on a tip'. However, since I was aware of the investors' hardships, I wanted to ensure I was not getting involved in a situation where I might have to arrest the investors for insider trading.

The following week, I happened to be in Ft. Worth, Texas. A Secret Service agent and I were interviewing a subject. The Secret Service was looking at Sam Clinton[28] on a counterfeit-currency case and I was conducting a bank fraud case on the same guy. After the attempted interview, I reached out to a contact of mine at the Securities and Exchange Commission (SEC). The regional office of the SEC is based in downtown Ft. Worth. Jason Smith[29] was an attorney with the SEC and a knowledgeable person who had assisted me in other investigations. I discussed the allegations with him. Smith smiled and disclosed that the SEC had received a complaint about HBLCO. Smith explained how since real estate was not a security, they did not act on the case. Smith assured me that investing in undeveloped land based on an inside tip was not insider trading. Putting this notion to rest, I continued with my investigation into the actions of Lucas Jr.

---

[28] Fictional name

[29] Fictional name

Chapter Fourteen
"HBLCO Insider"

With most cases, an agent always wants an insider within the company, organization, gang, 'ring', or other group, regardless of the type of criminal activity. The insider needs to be someone who is accessible, someone who can be trusted (at least to a point), and hopefully, someone who has not retained an attorney. I was looking for a weak link, someone who was involved with the Disney deals, someone who was not a member of the Lucas family, and someone who would qualify for a lesser plea based on the level of his cooperation with the government.

I considered Lucas Jr.'s father. However, I did not believe a father would provide incriminating information against his son. In fact, when I contacted his father, he declined to talk to the FBI.

I considered Uncle Chip but I came to the same conclusion that an uncle would not provide information against his nephew. After reading Uncle Chip's deposition, I realized Uncle Chip was all about saving his own skin. He threw Lucas, Jr. under the bus and denied knowing any of the Disney story was false. I talked to Uncle Chip in 2013. Despite all the evidence suggesting the Disney story was false, Uncle Chip—incredibly—still believed Disney would be building the theme park in North Texas. He did minimal due diligence because he simply did not want to know the story was false. There was money to be made in commissions and Uncle Chip realized this. During my interview with Uncle Chip, I discovered he was dying of cancer. Uncle Chip would later pass shortly after Lucas Jr.'s trial. Since my insider had to be someone who was not a member of the Lucas family, I made up my mind to pursue Mark Emerson as my HBLCO insider.

Emerson was a collegiate swimmer for SMU in the 1980s. SMU is located in Highland Park, which was considered one of the most prestigious neighborhoods in Dallas. Highland Park is located just north of downtown Dallas. This township was known as 'old money'. Emerson had a theological degree and no background in real estate. He was mentioned as one of the four individuals who conducted investor presentations.

Emerson met Uncle Chip in December 2005 through a swimming program in Dallas. Shortly after their meeting, Uncle Chip hired Emerson as a salesperson for HBLCO. My belief is Uncle Chip recruited Emerson because Emerson knew a lot of people in Highland Park—people with money who could afford to invest in a Disney theme park.

Emerson started his employment with HBLCO in January 2006. He was informed about Disney's plans to build a theme park in North Texas on his first day at work. Emerson was required to sign a non-disclosure agreement just like other investors to ensure he would not reveal the Disney secret to anyone not investing in land. After signing the non-disclosure agreement, Lucas Jr. and Uncle Chip told Emerson the details concerning the Disney theme park. Emerson was also told that Lucas Jr. had an insider at Disney who was supplying Lucas Jr. with confidential information. Emerson subsequently learned from Lucas Jr. that the name of the Disney source was Garrett

Singleton[30]. Lucas Jr. also showed Emerson a map of the Disney land acquisitions.

I chose to approach Emerson in January 2013. I had had allegations from investors suggesting Emerson was part of the scheme to defraud investors. He had made a few presentations and provided fraudulent documents to the investors including the fake Disney email reflecting his name in the distribution line. I was going into the interview believing Emerson was guilty of conspiracy to commit fraud. At the time, I had nothing more than testimony from witnesses. I needed a confession.

At the end of January 2013, DJ and I set out to conduct a "knock and talk" of Emerson. We knocked on the door but there was no answer. After some time at the front door of his condominium, there was still no answer, so we decided to leave. On the way out of the parking lot, we noticed several vehicles in the near proximity of Emerson's condo, so we started running license plate numbers. About the fourth vehicle run, the tag reflected it was registered to Emerson.

DJ and I returned to Emerson's front door and this time we pounded on the door identifying ourselves as the FBI. "Mr. Emerson, open the door or we'll sit by your car until you come out," I shouted. Eventually, Emerson answered his door with a dry head and crumbs on the side of his mouth. He apologized and said he was in the shower. Not only did I believe Emerson was culpable when I set out to interview him but now I was upset with him since I believed he was ducking us. DJ and I interviewed Emerson aggressively. We told him we considered him a subject in this fraud.

---

[30] Fictional name

Emerson confirmed he was a sales representative for HBLCO. He explained how he had become involved with HBLCO through Uncle Chip and how they knew each other through swimming. Uncle Chip knew Emerson had several contacts with money and could solicit some investors.

Emerson said he had participated in the investor presentations, but the presentations were mainly conducted by Lucas Jr. and Uncle Chip. We believed Emerson was minimizing his involvement, a tactic most criminals try. Emerson explained that at the presentations, the investors were shown different documents over the course of two years. They were shown concept plans, correspondence, an airport, a golf-course layout, a convention center, hotels, villas, multiple amusement parks, lease agreements with retailers, monorail design renderings, and advertisement posters. These documents were acquired from Lucas Jr. between 2006 and 2008.

Emerson vehemently denied participating in fraud and he said he had no knowledge of fraud occurring while he was at HBLCO. We knew this was not totally accurate since we knew Darius Garland had asked Emerson about the Photoshopped pictures of Jay Rasulo practicing his announcement speech at the Majestic Theatre, and the Photoshopped preliminary concept plan. Emerson had just lied to the FBI and possibly obstructed justice by misleading us. However, my experience has been that when the FBI shows up on someone's doorstep, it is not unusual for the interviewee to withhold information as a defense mechanism. I further believe that any agent or federal prosecutor who would charge someone with lying to the FBI without charging them with other substantive federal violations was either lazy, incompetent, sanctimonious, or all the above. After informing

Emerson of Mr. Garland's statement, Emerson rephrased his initial response about his knowledge of fraud by saying he heard Mr. Garland complain but he had not known about the photos until then. Emerson claimed he had immediately quit his job after he learned of Mr. Garland's allegation.

Emerson was then confronted with the email entitled "Fake Disney" in which he was on the distribution line. Emerson embarrassingly responded that the email was intended as a joke by Uncle Chip. Uncle Chip sent it to a local realtor who sold a lot of property in North Texas. The email was tied to a bet between Uncle Chip and the realtor. Based on what we knew at this point, Emerson's explanation of the email was unbelievable. But short of hitting him upside his head with a telephone book (which we do not do), we had to accept his answer until we could conduct further investigation. In the end, the "Fake Disney" email was somewhat of a paradox. It actually *was* a joke and not intended to be seen by the investors.

Emerson said he had had his doubts about the Disney theme park, but Uncle Chip kept telling him it was legitimate. Emerson confirmed that all the information regarding the theme park came from a Disney source who was a friend of Lucas Jr. Emerson explained his doubts had been based on the extraordinary story that Disney would actually build a theme park in North Texas, and the names of Lucas Jr.'s Disney source kept changing. First it had been Garrett Singleton, then George Owens, then someone named Chris, and then some unnamed guy who Lucas Jr. took to London. By the fall of 2008, Lucas Jr. said his Disney source had been getting his information from Bob Iger's and Jay Rasulo's secretaries. Also, the delayed announcements had been a concern to Emerson. He explained that everything had been tied to the announcement. Contract options were written in anticipation of the announcement. The announcement was necessary for all the investors to strike it big.

Emerson said announcement dates had moved from Thanksgiving 2006, to Super Bowl 2007, to Super Bowl 2008, to Fourth of July 2008, to the Olympic Games 2008, to October 2008. Emerson confirmed how he, Lucas Jr., Uncle Chip, and several other investors had gathered at one investor's residence to watch the 2007 Super Bowl. Emerson went on to describe what happened at that Super Bowl party, how none of the announcements were ever made, and how each time there was some excuse provided by Lucas Jr. Also, each time there would be some new document to keep the investors on the hook. The new document could be an email or an advertisement. But because the new information seemed plausible, all the investors, including him, accepted the excuses.

Even more convincing was the sales presentation he attended in the Spring 2008. He, Uncle Chip and Lucas Jr. flew to Indianapolis, Indiana to make a presentation to the Indianapolis Colts football team. Emerson figured that if Uncle Chip and Lucas Jr. were spending money to travel and make a presentation to such a public group, then this story had to be legitimate.

I asked Emerson what he was talking about when he said, "Including him." Emerson explained that he and his family members invested in the Disney deal because they believed all the representations made by Lucas Jr. They really believed Lucas Jr. had a source working for Disney. All the Emersons lost everything in the Disney deal. Emerson was being sued, he had gone through a divorce and he was on the verge of bankruptcy.

After the interview, I realized I had miscalculated the entire situation with Emerson. I went into the interview believing everyone selling property at HBLCO and making money off the Disney theme park information had some culpability. To me, this Disney story seemed so outrageous, I believed nobody could be this convinced. I eventually learned that there were victims inside of HBLCO as well as outside. My miscalculation could have made our case more difficult because Emerson retained an attorney after we left. I could have blown my opportunity of having an insider providing valuable information. However, in the end, Shamoil and I were able to convince Emerson's attorney that we believed Emerson and wanted his help as a witness for the government. As it turned out, Emerson made a darn good witness.

After this interview, I figured it would be more effective for me to wait on the subpoenaed bank records before interviewing more victims and potential subjects. However, by waiting, there would be a trade-off. I would lose overt criminal acts each week due to the 5-year statute of limitations expiring. In the meantime, I would focus on interviewing witnesses who were not victims.

Chapter Fifteen
"G'Man"

Lucas Jr. had identified his source's name to Uncle Chip in 2005. Initially, he stated his source was a longtime friend. After Uncle Chip asked numerous questions about the Disney source's identity, Lucas Jr. said the source was a high-school friend. Lucas Jr. subsequently said the friend did not actually attend the same high school as he did but that they graduated in the same year. After more pressure to identify the source, Lucas Jr. said his Disney source lived in Houston, Texas and worked for the Excalibur Management Group, the company responsible for buying land for Disney. Now to someone not involved in the Disney deal such as real-estate salespersons, investors, or someone else trying to make a dollar, this response might have made someone scratch their head. Why would someone who worked for Disney not live near Anaheim, California, Burbank, California or Orlando, Florida? Did the source work for Disney or a company dealing with Disney? I believe Uncle Chip was so focused because of the pot of gold at the end of the rainbow that he did not actually care about the identity as much as having a name to provide investors, if necessary. Finally, submitting to the constant questioning from Uncle Chip, Lucas Jr. identified his Disney source as "Garrett."

Through the review of records and interviews, I determined the two bogus letters written in 2005 between Ken Webb and

Jay Rasulo, and the Preliminary Concept Plan for Frontier Disney DFW were provided as attachments of an email chain, dated between September 2005 and October 2005, allegedly sent from email address garrett.singleton@gmail.com. At the end of one of the email messages, the author signed his name as G'Man. These three documents were the initial documents shown to investors to get them to invest their funds. They were also shown to investors at every investor presentation conducted by HBLCO.

Garrett Singleton worked for Excalibur Management Group from approximately October 2004 until approximately January 2006. He was allegedly the initial Disney source according to Lucas Jr. I located Mr. Singleton in Houston, Texas. In order to show a jury that all the representations made by Lucas Jr. were lies, I would have to interview all persons involved with each email, document, and photograph obtained. Accordingly, I contacted Mr. Singleton in Houston, Texas.

Mr. Singleton reviewed the email chain and confirmed that he had never seen the emails before. He confirmed that he neither sent the emails, received the emails, nor used the email address of garrett.singleton@gmail.com. Mr. Singleton defensively added that anyone could establish a gmail account. I sensed Mr. Singleton believed he might be a subject in the case so I reassured him that he was not a subject. Mr. Singleton said the "G'Man" reference sounded like someone trying to be cool.

After reviewing the letter dated May 21, 2005, from Ken Webb to Jay Rasulo, Mr. Singleton stated he never went to Hong Kong and did not know what the letter was regarding. Mr. Singleton said he was not even in the Dallas office of Excalibur Management Group. Mr. Singleton worked in the New York office. Mr. Singleton knew Ken Webb and knew Owen's last name was Owens. He was certain that neither Webb, nor Owens, went to Hong Kong because Excalibur Management Group did not have anything to do with Disney. Excalibur Management Group was a private equity firm and was not in the business of buying real estate.

Mr. Singleton had attended the bachelor party for Mitchell Robinson in Austin, Texas. He vaguely recalled Lucas Jr. being there but did not talk to him much. He thought Lucas Jr. was weird. Mr. Singleton certainly did not talk to Lucas Jr. after the bachelor party. He confirmed that the attendees of the bachelor party were all around the same age and consisted of pledge brothers of Dr. Robinson's and his high-school friends. Nobody named George Owens was at the bachelor party. Mr. Singleton had never heard of any talk related to Disney during the bachelor party.

Other participants of the bachelor party were interviewed. Each one testified predominantly the same as Mr. Singleton with regard to Lucas Jr. who was generally described as weird and a blowhard. A future brother-in-law of Dr. Robinson commented that he deliberately kept his distance from Lucas Jr. because of his lies. The future brother-in-law said Lucas Jr. had created a story that he was para-surfing in the Bahamas the entire month before the bachelor party. When asked why he thought this was a lie, the response was "because Lucas Jr. was so fat and out of shape, there was no way he could para-surf. There was also no tan on Lucas Jr. that would be associated with para-surfing or spending a month in the Bahamas." Another attendee of the bachelor party said Disney was never discussed among the group. The quote was, "We were at a bachelor party partying with naked dancing girls. Who would discuss business?"

Lucas Jr.'s lies were catching up to him. As announcement dates kept getting postponed, investors were demanding to know the identity of his Disney source. He. changed the identity of his source from Garrett Singleton to George Owens, who also worked at Excalibur Management Group. When George Owens left the Excalibur Management Group, Lucas Jr. had to concoct another name for the source. He then said his contact was "Chris", but could not recall his last name. I eventually reviewed a letter dated September 5, 2008, from Chris Lofton, Excalibur Management Group, to the Excalibur Management Group in Asia. I was able to determine this letter was fraudulent, too.

As things kept spinning out of control for Lucas Jr., he changed the names of the sources to Bob Iger's secretary, "Jennifer" and Jay Rasulo's secretary, "Sarah". I was able to determine that not only were these two names not the names of Lucas Jr.'s source(s) but neither Mr. Iger's secretary nor Mr. Rasulo's secretary were named Jennifer or Sarah. The names of all the named sources, to date, provided by Lucas Jr. between 2007 and 2009, were disprovable, with one exception. Lucas Jr. had informed Uncle Chip and Mark Emerson that he took his source to London in March 2007. Lucas Jr. refused to provide the name of this person. His reason was because he had made a promise to his source that he would never divulge his source's identity. Despite refusing to confirm the name of the source, Lucas Jr. was adamant the person he took to London was his Disney source. Lucas Jr. further confirmed that the money he was paid to entertain this person was spent on this London trip.

Above: Thomas Lucas, Jr. in London - March 2007 (Government exhibit)

*Above: AUSA Chris Eason and me at
Walt Disney Studios, Burbank, CA (Circa 2014)*

Above: Fraudulent advertisement photos of
DFW Disney announcement (Government exhibits)

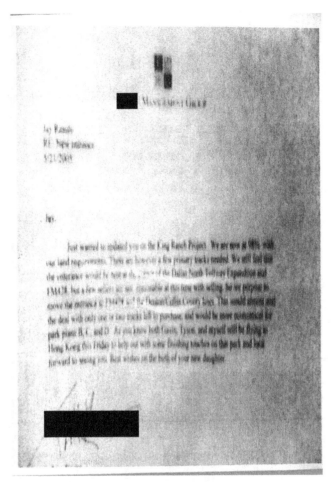

Above: Photo of blurred fraudulent letter from Ken Webb to Jay Rasulo — taken with investor's cell phone (Government exhibit)

EMG LOGO
MANAGEMENT GROUP

Jay Rasulo
RE: New entrance
5/21/2005

Jay,

Just wanted to updated you on the King Ranch Project. We are now at 98% with our land requirements. There are however a few primary tracks needed. We still feel that the entrance would be best at the corner of the Dallas North Tollway Expansion and FM428, but a few sellers are not reasonable at this time with selling. So we prepose to move the entrance to FM428 and the DentonCollin County lines. This would almost seal the deal with only one or two tracks left to purchase, and would be more economical for park plans B, C, and D. As you know both Gavin, Tyson, and myself will be flying to Hong Kong this Friday to help out with some finishing touches on that park and look forward to seeing you. Best wishes on the birth of your new daughter.

Vice President

LEE 001835

Above: Transcription of fraudulent letter from Webb (Government exhibit)

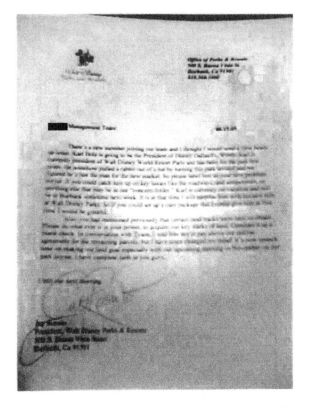

Above: Photo of blurred fraudulent letter from Jay Rasulo to Excalibur Management Team (Government exhibit)

Walt Disney
Parks and Resorts

Office of Parks & Resorts
500 S. Buena Vista St.
Burbank, Ca 91501
818.560.1000

██████Management Team: 08.15.05

There's a new member joining our team and I thought I would send a little heads
up letter. Karl Hotz is going to be President of Disney Dallas Ft. Worth. Karl is
currently president of Walt Disney World Resort Paris and has been for the past few
years. He somehow pulled a rabbit out of a hat by turning this park around and we
figured he's just the man for the new market. So please label him as your new problem
solver. If you could catch him up on key issues like the roadways, and temperature, or
anything else that may be in our "concern folder." Karl is currently on vacation and will
be in Burbank sometime next week. It is at that time I will surprise him with his new role
at Walt Disney Parks. So if you could set up a care package that I could give him at that
time I would be grateful.
    Also, you had mentioned previously that certain land tracks were hard to obtain.
Please do what ever is in your power, to acquire our key tracks of land. Consider it as a
blank check. In conversation with Tyson, I told him not to pay above our redline
agreement for the remaining parcels, but I have since changed my mind. It's now crunch
time in making our land goal, especially with our upcoming meeting in November on our
park layout. I have complete faith in you guys.

Until our next meeting,

Jay Rasulo
President, Walt Disney Parks & Resorts
500 S. Buena Vista Street
Burbank, Ca 91501

*Above: Transcription of fraudulent letter allegedly
written by Jay Rasulo (Government exhibit)*

*Above: Preliminary concept plan of Frontier Disney
(presented to investors) (Government exhibit)*

Prelimiary Concept Plan

FEBRUARY 8, 2006

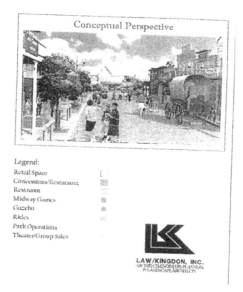

Conceptual Perspective

Legend:
Retail Space
Concessions/Restaraunt
Restroom
Midway Games
Gazebo
Rides
Park Operations
Theater/Group Sales

LAW/KINGDON, INC.
ARCHITECTS ENGINEERS, PLANNERS
& LANDSCAPE ARCHITECTS

Above: Preliminary concept plan of Wild West World
(Government exhibit)

Above: Photo of Jay Rasulo allegedly rehearsing an announcement speech for Frontier Disney at the Majestic Theatre, Dallas, Texas (provided to investors) (Government exhibit)

Above: Internet photo of Jay Rasulo at Disney's 50th Anniversary in New York City (50th Kick-off Coverage, Page 2) (n.d.) Retrieved April 03, 2018, from https://www.mouseplanet.com/7228/50thKickoffCoveragePage2 (Government exhibit)

Above: Photo of DFW Disney's Grand Texan Adventure shown to investors
(Government exhibit)

Above: Internet photo of Palazzo Del Lago Orlando Hotel (n.d.)
Retrieved from http://www.palazzodellago.com/ (Government exhibit)

Above: Fraudulent photo of Frontier Disney's Grand Texan Adventure
(Government exhibit)

Above:- Internet photo of Palazzo Del Lago (Palazzo del Lago Orlando Hotel
(n.d.) Retrieved from http://www.palazzodellago.com/ (Government exhibit)

Above left: SA John Skillestad clowning around in the squad area (Circa 2014)
Above right: SA Darrell James and me at SWAT training (Circa 2001)

Above: SA Steve Kleinlein and me waiting on a NASA tour
(NASA astronauts gave the FBI a private tour to show their appreciation for our
participation in the search for the Columbia Shuttle astronauts in 2003)

Chapter Sixteen
"Kaufman County Murders"

Kaufman County, Texas is located approximately 35 miles east of downtown Dallas. I considered any town 30 miles east of Dallas as East Texas, and bad things always seemed to happen in East Texas—hate crimes, methamphetamine cases, church arsons, small town government corruption, and murders. Kaufman County did have some nice qualities such as their fishing lakes and the Scarecrow Festival. However, it was still East Texas.

On January 31, 2013, I was organizing the Lucas Jr. case. A handful of agents were still in the office including Skilly and I. At around 6:00 pm we got a call from the Dallas Division Crisis Management supervisor. Skilly and I were informed that Kaufman County Assistant District Attorney (ADA) Mark Hasse had been murdered earlier that day. Since Skilly and I were both Deputy Crisis Managers, we were briefed on the situation.

After leaving the SWAT team in 2005, I needed some other interesting collateral duty that would give me a break from the paperwork associated with white-collar-crime cases. I joined Skilly on the Crisis Management Team. Crisis Management was responsible for establishing command posts and joint operation centers for various critical incidents and special events such as the Super Bowl, the NCAA Final Four, active shooter incidents, multi-agency arrests, kidnappings, and the murder of prosecutors. As part of this team, we were responsible for managing the investigative, intelligence, and situational awareness of the incident. This meant we were to ensure all tips and intelligence were documented and entered into our database; we ensured leads were assigned to investigators based on the tips; we ensured that the investigators provided a detailed and satisfactory report for the covered leads, and we ensured the case agent, Division management and Washington DC were frequently updated with the progress of the case.

The Crisis Management supervisor requested Skilly and me to get out to Kaufman County, establish liaison with the Kaufman County Sheriff's Office, and establish a Joint Operation Center (JOC). By the time Skilly and I had got to Kaufman County, the chaos of multi-agency investigations was already in full effect. Law enforcement officers from the state police (Department of Public Safety troopers and the Texas Rangers), Kaufman Police Department, Kaufman County Constable's Office, BATFE, DEA, and the FBI were all present. It is always inspiring to see so many dedicated officers respond to situations like this. However, the problem is always the same—officers are "running and gunning", that is, covering leads as fast as they can with little to no documentation. The problem with this is witnesses are contacted several times by different agencies, officers miss key facts, and witnesses are missed because one officer believes another officer contacted the witness. This was certainly true for this case. The job of Crisis Management is to establish an environment to ensure details are not missed.

Our initial JOC was in the Kaufman County mobile command post. This changed to the National Guard Armory the next morning due to the number of officers involved.

What we discovered once we arrived onsite was that ADA Hasse had been assassinated while walking from his car to the courthouse. The murderer had shot ADA Hasse repeatedly and then fled in an awaiting car. As usual, witnesses gave conflicting information regarding the murderer's description and the getaway car. Over the next couple of months, leads were exhaustingly covered. Speculation drove us in a direction to look at members of the Aryan Brotherhood, gang members, and past defendants who ADA Hasse had prosecuted, which included a man named Eric Williams.

Eric Williams was a former attorney and a former Justice of the Peace in Kaufman County. Williams had been prosecuted and publicly humiliated by ADA Hasse and District Attorney (DA) Mike McLelland for theft of a county computer. People around town knew of Williams' hatred towards the two prosecutors.

On March 30, 2013, we received information that DA McLelland and his wife were shot and killed in what was initially described as a home invasion assault. Numerous shells from a semi-automatic .223 rifle littered the floor of DA McLelland's home. Based on this evidence, we knew this was more than a home invasion; it was another assassination.

Through great investigative work by the lead investigators, the suspects were identified. On April 18, 2013, Eric Williams and his wife, Kim Williams were arrested for the three murders. The JOC was shut down shortly after.

Eric Williams was found guilty at trial and was subsequently sentenced to die by lethal injection. Kim Williams was found guilty in a separate trial and was sentenced to 40 years in prison.

After two months of working behind the scenes and 'skiing in the wake' of some dedicated and great investigators, I returned to the Lucas Jr. case knowing I had lost some valuable time and thus, criminal counts.

Chapter Seventeen
"Saving Taxpayer Dollars"

By the summer of 2013, a considerable amount of investigation had been conducted in a relatively short period of time. The Federal Grand Jury had provided the FBI with the necessary subpoenas to obtain the records we needed. Key witnesses such as Garrett Singleton—the initial Disney 'source'; Dennis Smith—president of the architecture firm Law Kingdon; a Disney executive who was knowledgeable about theme park developments; and Ken Webb—vice president of Excalibur Management Group, had all been interviewed and/or deposed through the civil lawsuits. Either way, relevant documented testimony had been obtained. Lucas Jr. was also deposed on several occasions. At this point, we believed we had enough evidence to prove our case-in-chief; that is, if Lucas Jr. went to trial, we had enough evidence to prove Lucas Jr. had committed wire fraud beyond a reasonable doubt.

At a minimum, we had the following direct or circumstantial evidence and testimony:

We had Ken Webb testifying that his signature on the letter dated May 21, 2005, from him to Jay Rasulo was a forgery, that he had not written the letter, and that Excalibur Management Group had never done business with Disney;

We had a deposition of a Disney executive who denied that Disney had plans to build a theme park in Texas;

We had the bogus photo of Jay Rasulo rehearsing his announcement speech at the Majestic Theatre in Dallas, which was a Photoshopped image taken from one of Mr. Rasulo's speech for Disney's 50th anniversary;

We had victims who would testify that Lucas Jr. was the person who 'obtained' the information from his source and who was the person who was making the investor presentations;

We had Mr. Singleton testifying that he did not really know Lucas Jr.; thought Lucas Jr. was weird; and never spoken to Lucas Jr. about Disney building a theme park; and

We had architect Dennis Smith who signed an affidavit reflecting he had never done any work for Disney and that the Concept Plans for Frontier Disney DFW were unauthorized reproductions of his Concept Plans for a theme park called Wild West World.

To save time and taxpayer dollars, we contacted Lucas Jr.'s attorney in August 2013, to request an interview with Lucas Jr. The interview would be conducted under a proffer letter. A proffer letter is an agreement between the target of the investigation and the government stating that none of the information provided by the potential subject could be used against him unless the subject lied. Some people refer to the proffer as the subject getting to be 'queen for a day'. We were cautious about Lucas Jr. telling the truth and the 'Larger Pinocchio' did not disappoint.

Chapter Eighteen
"Really, a Dead Guy?"

To prepare for the anticipated interview of Lucas, Jr., his civil depositions were reviewed by Shamoil and me. Inconsistencies within his depositions would be used in his interview. This would be his opportunity to set the record straight and to name his Disney source. It stood to reason that if he named a Disney source, then it might get him off the hook of being charged if he merely passed on bogus information.

Several telephone calls had been made between Lucas Jr.'s defense attorney, Jerry Williams[31], and Shamoil. We had made our case to Williams regarding the numerous inconsistencies made by Lucas Jr. to investors and during his civil depositions. Williams was informed that unless his client could tell the government the truth about the alleged Disney source, then Lucas Jr. would be indicted in September 2013. Williams was reminded that the name of the source had changed multiple times by his client to hide the true identity of the source. The source of the information had changed from an old friend, to a high-school friend, to a lifelong friend, to Garrett Singleton, to George Owens, to "Chris", to

---

[31] Fictional name

Bob Iger's secretary named Jennifer, and to Jay Rasulo's secretary named Sarah. We guaranteed Williams that unless we got the name of the source from Lucas Jr. or a confession that the source never existed, then Lucas Jr. would be indicted.

Williams took the government's intentions to his client. Lucas Jr. and he agreed to come in for an interview on the evening before our scheduled grand jury date to provide the government with the name of his Disney source. The agreement was that if Lucas Jr. was honest, Lucas Jr. would not be indicted the next day. Obviously, the reason for this was that the FBI would have to verify the information through interviews of the Disney source and other witnesses who knew the source. Additionally, we did not want to indict a person if that person was duped by someone else.

On September 10, 2013, Lucas Jr. and his attorney appeared at the United States Attorney's Office in Plano, Texas. Shamoil escorted them to the conference room B where I was waiting. I respectfully referred to this conference room as the Bradford Conference Room, which I unofficially named after Mike Bradford, a former US Attorney in the Eastern District of Texas. The room contained a long table which seated approximately 20 people. It also doubled as the law library for the prosecutors and interns.

Neither Shamoil nor I believed Lucas Jr. would tell us the truth based on past interviews of witnesses confirming his habitual lying, based on the evidence reviewed, and based on his testimony in his depositions. Moreover, Lucas Jr. had stated several times that when he gave his word to someone to keep their name confidential, he meant it. However, we had an ethical obligation to hear his voluntary statement. After some small talk between Williams and Shamoil, the meeting was turned over to me. I immediately told Lucas Jr. the meeting was a courtesy to him and that the reason we were in the room was to give him the opportunity to provide his side of the story. The meeting would also afford him the opportunity to provide the illusive name of his Disney source.

Lucas Jr. slowly leaned to his left and whispered something in his attorney's ear. After his attorney nodded, Lucas Jr. passed me an obituary he had printed from the Internet along with a photo he had taken with his cell phone. The obituary was for a man named Paul Johnson. The obituary reflected that Johnson had died on January 1, 2012, at the age of 66. I would later learn that Johnson's death was from a suicide. Lucas 'admitted' that Johnson was his Disney source. This 66-year-old gentleman was obviously not "someone Lucas Jr. went to high school with." As I was passing the obituary to Shamoil, I looked across the table straight into Lucas Jr.'s eyes and sarcastically said, "Really Thomas, you're giving us the name of a dead guy?" As I looked at Williams, I could see embarrassment on his rose-colored face. I have no doubt Lucas Jr. provided us the name of Johnson because he believed there was no way for us to disprove Johnson was the Disney source. I also have no doubt that Lucas Jr. scheduled his interview the night before he was supposed to be indicted to delay the indictment for another month, a delay distinctly consistent with the way all the alleged Disney announcements were 'delayed'.

We attempted to question Lucas Jr. regarding Johnson's access to Disney and why Lucas Jr. had not previously provided this name in his civil depositions or to the FBI. Lucas Jr. responded, "When I give my word to a friend to keep his name confidential, I keep my word." We asked Lucas Jr. if keeping his word to someone who was no longer alive was worth going to jail. "Yes, it is," was the response.

"Why would anyone spend thousands of dollars on attorneys to represent you and your family in criminal and civil matters when the lawsuits could go away by just naming the Disney source", I asked. Lucas Jr. robotically repeated his pledge of confidentiality he claimed to have given to Johnson.

After Lucas Jr. provided us the name of Johnson, I undoubtedly believed this was just another one of Lucas Jr.'s lies. There was a good chance that everything Lucas Jr. said in the interview would also be a lie so his statements could all be used against him for violating the terms of his proffer agreement.

Lucas Jr. said he had met Johnson at Mitchell Robinson's bachelor party in Austin, Texas in 2005. He said one of the bachelor party events was tubing down the Guadalupe River. While driving to the river, Dr. Robinson's future brother-in-law had brought up the topic of Disney building a theme park in Celina, Texas. I had already interviewed both of Dr. Robinson's brothers-in-law, so I knew neither person had any knowledge about a Disney rumor. Lucas Jr. said little else was discussed about Disney until that evening.

He then went on to say that evening (the Saturday), the bachelor party had gone to a well-known local strip club called PTAX[32]. This is where Johnson started talking about Disney. Lucas Jr. said there must have been between 75 and 100 people at the bachelor party. The only person that Lucas Jr. knew at the table with him and Johnson was Garrett Singleton. In response to a question, Lucas Jr. said that if Mr. Singleton denied hearing about the Disney theme park while at the table, then Mr. Singleton was lying. Lucas Jr. was continuing his lies. We knew the bachelor party went to PTAX on Friday night and there was not more than 15 people at the party. Also, Mr. Singleton had already denied hearing about

---

[32] Fictional name

Disney or really knowing Lucas Jr. However, instead of interrupting Lucas Jr., I felt it was better to let him dig a deeper grave. He certainly was burying himself!

While at PTAX, Johnson allegedly told Lucas Jr. that he had a "friend" who knew about the Disney theme park being built in North Texas. Johnson did not provide any detailed information about the "friend" at Disney. However, Johnson purportedly showed Lucas Jr. a Disney business card that said "George something" on it. Lucas Jr. said he did not recall George's last name. This was interesting because Lucas Jr. was naming Johnson as the Disney source and then alluding to George as being the Disney source.

Lucas Jr. informed us that after the bachelor party, he did not hear from Johnson again until October 2005. This was also interesting to us because we believed Lucas Jr. should have seen Johnson at the wedding and as excited as Uncle Chip was about the Disney news, it was logical to presume Uncle Chip would have pushed Lucas Jr. to extract more information from Johnson while at the wedding.

In October 2005, Johnson supposedly contacted Lucas Jr. and told him that he (Johnson) was in Dallas and wanted to discuss Disney. We determined later that Johnson was in Dallas because he was a Hurricane Katrina victim. (In late August 2005, New Orleans was hit by one of the most devastating hurricanes in US history. Numerous victims relocated to the Dallas area because of the severe flooding in New Orleans. Johnson was one of these victims.)

Lucas Jr. was questioned about his method of contact with Johnson. Lucas Jr. responded that he never met Johnson in person.

Johnson gave him burner phones to use. (Burner phones are pre-paid cell phones, widely used by drug distributors.) When the phone reached its limited minutes, Lucas Jr. claimed he threw away the cell phone and Johnson gave him a new prepaid cell phone. He said he did not recall any of Johnson's cell phone numbers and he claimed not to have them saved in his cell phone.

"If you and Johnson were not meeting in person, then how was Johnson providing you the phones?" was the obvious next question. Lucas Jr. stared at me for a moment. I could see he was formulating his next lie but he had no initial response. Lucas Jr. then said they would meet at Starbucks or restaurants in order for Lucas Jr. to get the phone. They also allegedly once met at a hotel in Addison, Texas, which is another suburb of Dallas.

The obvious follow-up question was how Lucas Jr. would know when and where to meet. He informed us that Johnson would send him an email when he wanted to meet or when he had new documents to provide. However, he conveniently could not recall Johnson's email address, saying that Johnson kept changing his email address so there was no way to recall the email addresses. Lucas Jr. said the emails and email addresses could not be retrieved from his laptop either because the hard drive was "fried" so he had disposed of his laptop. He told us it would not have done any good to search his laptop because he and Johnson exchanged emails without sending them. He explained he and Johnson were both able to log onto the email account to draft and read the emails. After the receiving party read the draft email, the receiver deleted the draft. This way nothing was ever sent or memorialized.

I was thinking about how all of Lucas Jr.'s high school friends had described Lucas Jr. as full of crap. The method of communicating through draft emails is how the terrorists who crashed planes into the World Trade Center twin towers, the Pentagon, and an empty field in Pennsylvania (United Flight 93), all communicated. Lucas Jr.'s story was ridiculous. He continued to tell one lie after another. At best, he seemed to be delusional and living in some kind of international spy fantasy world, using burner phones, draft emails, and sneaking around back alleys.

Lucas Jr. described how the flow of Disney information went from George to Johnson to him. He restated he could not recall George's last name. Lucas Jr. confirmed that he then provided the Disney information to his Uncle Chip and other salespersons at HBLCO. He also confirmed he had made presentations to investors and used the Disney information to solicit the investors. Lucas Jr. also said he had never provided Johnson's name to the investors. He had merely told them he got the Disney information from a friend of a friend.

Lucas Jr. confirmed that Johnson had specifically told him that Disney was buying up land at FM 428 and the Dallas North Tollway. The land was being purchased under a straw buyer so the theme park would remain a secret. He identified the straw buyer as Excalibur Management Group and said "George" worked for this group. I found it interesting that Lucas Jr. previously gave up George but not Johnson. I concluded this was just a simple case of not realizing the implications of one's own lies or not being able to keep one's lies straight.

Lucas Jr. continued with his story… Johnson was supposedly providing the information to Lucas Jr. because he liked him and was just trying to help Lucas Jr. make some money. A revelation came to me while Lucas Jr. was talking about Johnson and how Johnson wanted no money for his actions. Lucas Jr. had possibly created an imaginary friend because he actually craved a genuine relationship with someone. He had soured all his previous friendships due to his habitual lying. The only way he could convince us about this whole story was to convince us of the generosity of his friend and that his friend was legitimate. This tactic is not unusual for criminals. It is a way of minimizing their involvement in a crime. The rationale is if one can direct law enforcement's attention to another person or persons, then perhaps he looks less guilty. Shamoil and I had no intention of trusting Lucas Jr. This was just another lie. I sat in the interview and thought about how Lucas Jr. met this 66-year-old Hurricane Katrina refugee at a bachelor party for 20-year-old kids. The fact of the matter was, I thought, *Pinocchio's larger twin was a clown.*

Lucas Jr. was questioned about his presentations to the investors. He claimed that he always did three things prior to the presentations. One, he provided the investors with a book called "Disneyland That Never Worked"; two, he told the investors there was risk involved with the project; and three, he told the investors that the land deals were a "Dallas North Tollway play" first and Disney was an added bonus to the investment. Lucas Jr. implied that since the Dallas North Tollway had expanded north from downtown Dallas through Addison, Plano, and Frisco, and since the plans were for the tollway to expand all the way through Celina, Texas up to the Oklahoma border, then the land would be worth a lot of money someday. What Lucas Jr. did not explain was that if the land deals were hinged on the Dallas North Tollway, then why did all the Power Point slides made at the investor presentations deal with Disney, and not the tollway? Furthermore, why were the option contracts short-termed and tied to the Disney announcement?

Lucas Jr.'s explanation was ridiculous because the tollway expansion was years away (as of the writing of this book, the tollway still hasn't moved past Frisco, Texas—15 years after the initial real estate sale was made). By this time, I had become frustrated with Lucas Jr.'s lies. I knew everything he was saying could easily be confirmed as being a lie except for Johnson's relation to this story. Lucas Jr. adamantly believed there was no way the FBI could prove Johnson was not the Disney source, which is why he chose to throw Johnson under the bus. He was confident and smug in the delivery of his lies.

It was getting late in the evening. My impatience grew with every breath this morally corrupted kid took. However, we let him continue. We also attempted to get as much information about Johnson as possible. Lucas Jr. said that when Johnson first got to the Dallas area in 2005, Johnson lived with his sister-in-law. He subsequently moved to Frisco, Texas. He used to be a milk delivery man and he used to sell cars. By this time, Lucas Jr.'s stories were becoming comical. I asked Lucas Jr., "Did you ever see any red flags with an anonymous Katrina refugee who delivered milk, who you met at a strip club during a bachelor party, and who wanted to provide you with second-hand information about Disney building a theme park in North Texas? All this because he wanted to help a guy, whom he had just met, make some money?"

Lucas Jr. responded, "I did not." He added that if he had thought the information regarding Disney was bogus, neither he nor his family members would have invested in Lucas Celina 209 or some of the other deals. This was a futile argument because Lucas Celina 209 was collateralized with 209 acres of land, which meant the land could be sold at a gain or to minimize any losses. As for the "other deals" Lucas Jr. and his family members invested in, these were one-percent contractual ownership interests they received for selling the land; no money came from their own pockets.

As the interview continued, Lucas Jr.'s responses regarding the Disney source lessened with respect to George providing the information and increased regarding Johnson being the source. Lucas Jr. said that if he stated in his deposition that he graduated with the source, then this was false since obviously he could not have graduated with Johnson. Again, providing us with the name of Johnson as the source was contradicting his own statements in his deposition. This always plays out great at trial, such as, "Are you lying here in trial or were you lying in your deposition?" Lucas Jr. also confirmed he took Johnson to London. The money used for the London trip was apparently paid with the commissions Lucas Jr. made on the land deals.

I showed Lucas Jr. the poorly written 2005 letters between Jay Rasulo and Ken Webb. When I asked him if the letters were false, he responded he got them from Johnson and did not know whether they were false. I then asked Lucas Jr. to spell the word "tract" which was misspelled as "track" in both letters. Lucas Jr. stared at me like the proverbial deer in the headlights. He then refused to spell the word.

Again, Lucas Jr. knew he could not provide the name of a living person as his Disney source because he knew that the FBI could determine, without a doubt, that the whole matter about Disney building a theme park in North Texas was a lie. The alleged Disney source was someone Lucas Jr. knew who would be able to expose his misrepresentations beyond a reasonable doubt. Lucas Jr.'s mistake was that he thought he was smarter than the rest of the world. I took some satisfaction in telling Lucas Jr. I thought he was "full of shit" before escorting him out of the office.

Lucas Jr. was indicted the next day on four counts of wire fraud. Obviously, there were more counts, but the government only had to prove one count to send him to jail. The four counts selected were the easiest to prove at trial.

Chapter Nineteen
"A New Kid in Town"

Lucas Jr. pleaded "not guilty" at his arraignment. This was no surprise because in 25 years in law enforcement, I never saw anyone enter a guilty plea at their arraignment. In fact, I worked a civil rights case (a hate crime) on a pair of church arsons in Greenville, Texas, which was jointly investigated with the Bureau of Alcohol, Tobacco, Firearms and Explosives; the Texas Rangers; and the Greenville Police Department. Since the church's congregation was African American, the case was investigated as a hate crime. One day during the church arson investigation, Greenville Police Officer Murphy Morris[33] and I were on our way to interview a witness. We were detoured by the police department dispatcher who was calling Officer Morris to inform him that a murder had just occurred. Officer Morris and I went "code" (lights, siren, 100 mph) to the crime scene. As Officer Morris and I entered the crime scene, we were told by witnesses the murderer had calmly walked down to the police station which was approximately four blocks away. We were concerned because he had taken the firearm used to murder the victim. We later learned from Sergeant Larry Knox[34], Criminal Investigative Division (CID), that the murderer walked

---

[33] Fictional name

[34] Fictional name

straight into his office, handed over the weapon, and confessed to killing the victim. The murderer said to Sergeant Knox, "Larry, I killed him. He pissed me off and I shot him dead." Even though this confession was video recorded, the murderer still pleaded "not guilty" at his arraignment. Now only a great legal mind can explain to me why there was a "not guilty" plea at the arraignment, but my cynical suspicion was so some defense attorney somewhere could make enough money to make the next mortgage payment on his vacation home.

After his arraignment, Lucas Jr. was released on his own recognizance. This is a situation where defendants are allowed to stay out of jail until their trial, providing they comply with the conditions imposed by the United States Magistrate Judge.

Soon after the arraignment, my good friend Shamoil confided in me that he was provided with the opportunity to continue his legal career in private practice at a prestigious law firm in Dallas. I was extremely happy for Shamoil but at the same time, I was sad to be losing our investigator-prosecutor relationship. I jokingly compare Shamoil's departure before the case was finished to a situation where he and I took a trip to the Grand Canyon, and while I was admiring all its glory, Shamoil drove away in the car. He asked who I wanted to go to trial with in the Disney matter. There was no hesitation with my response. I immediately answered, "Eason."

—————————

When AUSA Chris Eason first came to the United States Attorney's Office (a couple of years before the Lucas Jr. case), he unknowingly and unintentionally upset me. Shamoil and I were preparing for trial on one of the biggest mortgage fraud cases in the country. We indicted 40 persons, of which all but three eventually pleaded guilty.

Indicting this many persons on one white-collar case is extremely unusual. The three remaining persons going to trial included an appraiser, a mortgage broker and a mortgage loan officer.

One day Shamoil brought Eason into one of the conference rooms and introduced him to me. I was informed that Eason would not only be helping with the mortgage trial, but also that Eason would be the prosecutor who questioned me on the witness stand. As Eason and I prepared for my line of questioning, he started 'cross examining' me like I was the one on trial, which kind of irked me. I recall thinking he was an exceptional 'defense attorney'; the only problem being, he was supposed to be the prosecutor. I paused the trial preparation, went into Shamoil's office and said, "Why the heck do you have this 'kid' doing my direct examination?" After discussing the matter further, Shamoil agreed to question me when I took the witness stand.

Preparing for this mortgage fraud case occupied a considerable amount of time. We were working evenings, weekends, and holidays to get ready for the trial. During this time of preparation, Eason and I developed a great friendship. We learned about each other's personal and professional lives. In fact, on the evening of July 4th, while working on the trial, my wife and daughter surprised us by bringing some good ole Texas BBQ to the United States Attorney's Office. We all chowed down on brisket, sausage and turkey while watching fireworks from the conference room on the fifth floor of the building.

Eason is a guy who grew up on the 'south side' of Oklahoma City, or, some might say, the rough part of town. This meant he had faced some of the same challenges I had; challenges that others in his position would not understand. He had washed dishes to earn money during his undergraduate years. He had served in the Air Force and continues to serve our country in the Air Force reserves within the Judge Advocate General's (JAG) Office. He has successfully tried cases involving international terrorism in extraterritorial locations and his resume is long and distinguished. But his one true quality, and what impressed me most, is his junk-yard dog character. The 'south side' attitude of Eason does not allow him to back down from a fight. Whereas most prosecutors do not challenge judges, he has challenged judges on their misunderstanding and misinterpretation of the law on numerous occasions. Not only are his challenges of judges impressive but sometimes even comically entertaining, especially when he is scolded by a federal judge, who knows he/she (judge) is always the biggest dog in the yard.

Once Lucas Jr. was arraigned, the real work started. During the pre-indictment phase of the investigation, the investigator calls the shots on how the case will progress. However, during the post-indictment phase, the investigator should do what the prosecutor needs to get ready for trial. In this case, Eason wanted additional victims interviewed and he wanted Disney representatives interviewed. Since photos of Jay Rasulo had been Photoshopped and since Mr. Rasulo and Bob Iger's signatures were forged, Eason wanted both of them interviewed. Keep in mind, Mr. Iger and Mr. Rasulo were the number one and number two guys in charge of Disney. Mr. Iger was the present day "Walt Disney" and Mr. Rasulo was the present day "Roy Disney"; they were synonymous with "Mickey Mouse and Donald Duck"; they were the heavy hitters at Disney. Eason also wanted the obvious—to determine whether Paul Johnson was the Disney source and whether he traveled to London with Lucas Jr. Finally, Eason wanted to supersede the indictment to increase the wire fraud counts, add detail to the counts already charged and to include a charge of lying to the FBI.

Chapter Twenty
"Hurricane Katrina"

With the assistance of a loyal and trusted friend, Michele Miller, we went to work on developing background information regarding Paul Johnson. Miller was a support technician who assisted the agents in the RA with various tasks, such as, locating subjects and witnesses, serving document subpoenas, running criminal histories on people, and conducting Internet research, to name a few helpful functions. She had a great demeanor and an outstanding work ethic. She was also fun to kid around with.

Miller conducted the research on Johnson using only his approximate age. She looked for persons in the New Orleans area prior to August 2005 (Hurricane Katrina) and she compared possible people to the Johnsons in the Dallas area after August 2005. She came up with several addresses for me to check.

Early next morning, I went 'hunting'. I knocked on several doors of the potential addresses that Michele had located as possible persons who might know Paul Johnson. I left my business card at several residences but received no return phone calls. Finally, on the last address, I went to an apartment complex in Frisco, Texas. As was customary, I went into the leasing office to speak with one of the young ladies. In 25 years with the FBI, I have found that there is not one young lady in her 20s who doesn't want to meet an FBI agent. Even more, a well-mannered FBI agent in a suit, wearing a badge on his belt and a smile on his face will always get the leasing manager to open her files to the FBI agent. "Bingo", the file for apartment #2118 reflected Lorena Barr as the tenant. Ms. Barr reflected a cell phone number with an area code from New Orleans. She also showed a previous address in New Orleans. I went to the apartment and gently knocked on her door but there was no answer. I left a card with the intention of returning the next morning. However, later that evening, I received a telephone call from a polite southern lady identifying herself as Lorena Barr.

Ms. Barr was an extremely nice person, somewhere in her 60s and had a mild Cajun accent. She was a total lady and very likable. She agreed to talk to me about her common law husband, Paul Johnson. Ms. Barr informed me she had been with Johnson for over 25 years. She knew him better than anyone. When I asked her about Johnson's prior jobs which I learned from Lucas Jr., she was quick to tell me about his milk delivery job and his car salesman job. This was sort of a test to determine the level of reliability which I could put in her testimony.

Ms. Barr confirmed she and Johnson came to the Dallas area in 2005, because of Hurricane Katrina destroying their home in New Orleans. She said she was with Johnson the entire time after relocating and denied ever living with Johnson's sister, as stated by Lucas Jr. Ms. Barr said Johnson's sister did not even live in the Dallas area.

I asked Ms. Barr if she knew a person named Thomas Lucas, Jr. "Yeah, I know Tom," said Ms. Barr. She had never met Lucas Jr., but Johnson mentioned Lucas Jr. on several occasions. Johnson described Lucas Jr. to Ms. Barr. "Tom was a chunky white male who was full of crap." Johnson also described Lucas

Jr. as a "shyster" and a "bullshitter." Johnson had conveyed to Ms. Barr that Lucas Jr. was always exaggerating the truth. Ms. Barr explained that Johnson had met Lucas Jr. at a methadone rehabilitation clinic.

Ms. Barr said Johnson was never involved with anything pertaining to Disney. Johnson had never worked for Disney or on behalf of Disney. She said Johnson had never traveled to London in 2007, or any other time. Johnson did not have a passport, nor did he travel anywhere with Lucas Jr. She also stated Johnson had never used prepaid cell phones. Ms. Barr sorrowfully stated her husband passed on January 1, 2012.

Before I departed down the exterior stairwell, Ms. Barr said she had kept Johnson's cell phone and wallet. She maintained these items as keepsakes and assured me she had maintained their content the same way as the day Johnson passed. We plugged the phone into a charger and reviewed the limited cell phone contact list together. Lucas Jr. was in the contact list along with a couple of other names that were not George Owens, or Kyle, or Garrett Singleton, or Mitchell Robinson, or anyone else at Disney. We reviewed the limited content of the wallet which did not contain anything related to Disney including any business cards referencing Disney.

We had just proven that everything Lucas Jr. had blamed on Johnson was a lie. Johnson had nothing to do with Disney; therefore, he was not the Disney source. It was also confirmation that Lucas Jr. had lied to the FBI.

Eason superseded the original indictment to add three more counts of wire fraud and one count of Title 18 U.S.C., Section 1001, False Statements (for lying to the FBI). I laughed at this final charge of lying to the FBI because I am not a fan of using this statute; however, since it was being charged with the wire fraud violations, I did not make a big deal about it. I jokingly told Eason that if we were going to charge one count of lying to the FBI, we might as well charge a thousand counts; one count for each time Lucas Jr. opened his mouth.

We still had a question we wanted answered by trial. Who was the mystery person that Lucas Jr. took to London?

Chapter Twenty-One
"Rounding out the Witnesses for Trial"

Eason wanted another high-profile witness for trail. We selected Jay Underwood[35], a former player in the National Football League (NFL) who was currently residing in the Philadelphia area. Mr. Underwood was contacted to schedule an interview. He did not want to meet at his office for an undisclosed reason. I assumed it was either because he was embarrassed about his financial loss which is not unusual for victims of investment schemes, or he did not want his co-workers knowing he was talking to a law enforcement officer. We agreed to meet in the hotel bar area of the Embassy Suites near the airport. I hurriedly packed a bag and caught the next flight to Philadelphia.

Mr. Underwood was an amazing player at a historically powerhouse college football program in the late 1980s. He was a two time All-American and part of a National Championship team. In 1991, he was drafted by a professional team and played ten years with the organization. He was an NFL All-Pro for several years and a member of an NFL Championship team.

Sometime in 2007, Mr. Underwood was contacted by his childhood friend, Mark Emerson. They had played sports and

---

[35] Fictional name and stats of professional athlete

grown up in Alexandria, Virginia together. Emerson solicited Mr. Underwood to invest in Celina 209, which was the purchase of actual land. In approximately August 2007, Mr. Underwood invested a couple hundred thousand dollars in this project.

Shortly after this initial investment, Mr. Underwood was re-contacted by Emerson, Lucas Jr. and Uncle Chip regarding investing his money in land option contracts. The details of the solicitation were consistent with those given to the other investors. Lucas Jr. had a friend inside of Disney who said Disney was planning to build a theme park in North Texas. Mr. Underwood was interested but he wanted to see what was happening for himself. Mr. Underwood traveled to Texas to attend a presentation given by Lucas Jr. He recalled Darius Garland being at the presentation which stood out in his mind since they were both professional athletes. Lucas Jr.'s presentation was an elaborate slide show which included an aerial map, documents with Disney logos, letters by Disney executives, and rides. Mr. Underwood recalled the airport that would be built which included a monorail that would travel from the airport to the theme park. At the presentation, Lucas Jr. confirmed his source worked at Disney; however, Lucas Jr. would not reveal the source's name.

After the presentation, Mr. Underwood and Emerson drove out to the location where Frontier Disney was supposed to be built. Mr. Underwood viewed the land he had initially invested in and the proposed properties discussed in the presentation.

Based on Lucas Jr.'s presentation, Mr. Underwood invested an additional $100,000 to $150,000 in the Old 686 Joint Venture and the OHOAD Joint Venture. Each joint venture purchased land option contracts. Mr. Underwood wanted to get his money into the projects prior to the anticipated announcement during the 2008 Super Bowl. However, Mr. Underwood also described how this announcement and all the subsequent planned announcements were delayed. By the time Mr. Underwood became uncomfortable with the delayed announcements, Emerson had left HBLCO. Mr. Underwood did not suspect his friend of fraud. He believed Emerson was duped just like everyone else.

Like the other investors, Mr. Underwood's investments in the land option contracts were a total loss.

———————————————

I re-interviewed the attendees of the bachelor party to determine whether anyone there recalled Paul Johnson, a 60-year-old man, or anyone named George Owens being there. All the responses were the same. Johnson was not there, nobody named George Owens was there, and there was certainly not a 60-year-old man there. The main two attendees, Mitchell Robinson (bachelor) and Garrett Singleton (Excalibur Management Group employee) also confirmed Johnson and George Owens were not there.

Dr. Robinson knew everyone at the bachelor party, as well he should have. He emphatically denied knowing anyone named Johnson or George Owens.

Since Lucas Jr. had indicated George worked at Excalibur Management Group, Mr. Singleton was a key witness. Mr. Singleton knew the identity of George Owens. Mr. Singleton emphatically stated that neither George Owens nor anyone from Excalibur Management Group, attended the bachelor party.

During the re-interview of Brian Mattingly, I honed in on something that had previously escaped me. If you recall, Mattingly was at the bachelor party. He was also a high-school friend of Lucas Jr.'s. Since they were high-school friends, he too had experienced Lucas Jr.'s past history of lies. Mattingly was currently employed in the software industry and was familiar with Lucas Jr.'s mastery with computers. I questioned Mattingly about what it would take to create the fake conceptual plans, the fake photo of Jay Rasulo on stage, and the fake Disney logos. Mattingly explained that all a person would need is Adobe software and to know his way around the software. Mattingly confirmed Lucas Jr. had computer-aided design software on his computer because Mattingly had seen it. Computer-aided design software allowed someone to create architectural designs, floor plans, theme park plans, golf course plans, etc. After the interview, I went back to my office and reviewed Lucas Jr.'s bank records. In the records I located a $2,000 purchase of Adobe software. The date of the purchase coincided with the date when the preliminary concept plan was initially presented. Now, this is not evidence of anything, really. However, it is one more piece of a large puzzle that circumstantially shows a link between Lucas Jr. and Photoshopped pictures. It showed Lucas Jr. had the opportunity and access to create the false photos and records he was showing the investors.

A final question asked of Lucas Jr.'s friends was whether Lucas Jr. had solicited them to invest in the Frontier Disney scam. Not one friend was solicited. This was revealing because if Lucas Jr.'s Frontier Disney story was legitimate, then why not solicit your closest friends so they also could make some money? The answer is because none of them would have invested money in any of Lucas Jr.'s ideas since they knew his track record of being unable to tell the truth. This was unfortunate because if any of them had been solicited, then perhaps they would have called Lucas Jr. out and saved investors millions of dollars.

Eason requested me to follow up on an email Lucas Jr. had distributed to others within HBLCO. As you may recall, Lucas Jr. attempted to use Mattingly as a witness when he tried planting the seed of the Disney theme park in Mattingly's head while at the bachelor party. He also tried doing the same thing with another old friend from high school. The old friend was Kendall Kent, a news anchor with one of the Dallas News stations.

Lucas Jr. had bumped into Ms. Kent at a local mall. He asked Ms. Kent if she heard about Disney building the theme park in North Texas. Ms. Kent responded she had heard that rumor for years and there was nothing to it. However, Lucas Jr. memorialized the chance meeting with Ms. Kent in an email to his father and uncle (previously referenced). Lucas Jr. claimed Ms. Kent was attending a meeting with Disney executives in Dallas where they were discussing the upcoming Disney announcement.

After ensuring the attorneys at the local news station that my interview had nothing to do with their brand, they allowed Ms. Kent to be interviewed. Ms. Kent was an attractive lady. Her chestnut-colored hair extended to her shoulders and her nervous green eyes stared at me as though she was looking into the news camera. I showed her the email. After reading the content of the email, her nervousness dissipated and turned to a controlled anger. She was noticeably upset. She said the email was inaccurate and false. She furiously denied she had conveyed to Lucas Jr. that she was attending a meeting with Disney, and she confirmed Lucas Jr. had been a liar ever since she knew him.

--- --- ---

The Excalibur Management Group employees were next on our interview list. We had already nailed down Mr. Singleton's testimony, which would be convincing at trial. However, we wanted no wiggle room for Lucas Jr.

I contacted Ken Webb, Vice President of Excalibur Management Group. Webb was the person who allegedly wrote and received the letters to and from Jay Rasulo. He was certainly a person in a position to know the company's business strategy.

Webb informed me that their company acquired distressed companies and turned those companies around to make them profitable. Making land purchases was not a part of Excalibur Management Group's business. Webb stated Excalibur Management Group never acquired land for themselves, nor for Disney.

Webb reviewed the letter dated May 21, 2005. Not only did Webb deny writing the letter, but he also confirmed his signature was a forgery. Webb also described the letter as the worst business letter he had ever read, and he questioned how any person could have invested their hard-earned money after reading this poorly written letter. Webb boldly stated, "Excalibur Management Group has had no affiliation with Disney."

--- --- ---

With Michele Miller's assistance again, we were able to locate George Owens, former employee of Excalibur Management Group.

Owens was one of the names that Lucas Jr. used to identify his Disney source. We located Owens in Chicago, Illinois and interviewed him. As anticipated, Owens did not know Lucas Jr. and did not recognize the photo of Lucas Jr. Owens did not know Mitchell Robinson and never attended a bachelor party for Dr. Robinson. Owens never conducted business with, for or on behalf of Disney. Owens also never told anyone that Disney was going to build a theme park in North Texas.

There were a few questions we never got an answer to. Owens worked for Excalibur Management Group between 2003 and 2005. Mr. Singleton and Webb worked for Excalibur Management Group. One of the questions never answered was how Lucas Jr. chose Excalibur Management Group as the company acting as the secret purchaser of land on behalf of Disney. This will remain a mystery; however, I believe when Lucas Jr. met Singleton at the bachelor party, Singleton introduced himself as someone who worked for Excalibur Management Group. As for the employees, I am certain Lucas Jr. merely conducted a search on the Internet of the company and used the company's website to identify the employees.

———————————————

As you can see, Lucas Jr. not only victimized the investors, but he also victimized other persons, including witnesses who had nothing to do with Lucas Jr.'s scam—nothing other than having their name or brand unknowingly used by Lucas Jr. to effect his scheme.

A typical white-collar case will involve witnesses who usually add knowledge to the case, such as information against the defendant. However, in this case, Lucas Jr. told so many lies and fictional alibis that we had to prove the negative. What I mean by this is we had to interview witnesses to get them to say they had no knowledge of anything. These witnesses had to leave their jobs two or three times to be interviewed by the government. Then they had to leave their job, city, and state to appear at a trial in Sherman, Texas. These witnesses were doctors, teachers, business persons, news anchors, etc. And because they had to leave their jobs, the people they dealt with were also affected; all because some conman desired recognition and status by concocting a fictional story about Disney just to feed his own ego and diminish his own inadequacies.

Chapter Twenty-Two
"500 South Buena Vista"

I reviewed numerous depositions in this case. One was of a witness, Stanley Mazor[36], Vice President of Animal Kingdom for Walt Disney Parks and Resorts. Mazor had testified in his deposition that Disney had no intention of building a theme park in North Texas. He also testified that Disney did not have a contract with Excalibur Management Group to purchase land for Disney. This was good information, but we needed someone higher up the corporate food chain from Disney. The two individuals we had in mind were Robert Iger, Chairman and Chief Executive Officer for the Walt Disney Company and Jay Rasulo, Chief Financial Officer for the Walt Disney Company. Since these two Disney executives' names had been forged on documents and since their knowledge of any planned theme parks would be unrefuted, they were the ones we had to interview. So, Eason and I set off for the Walt Disney Company, 500 South Buena Vista, Burbank, California.

Now, not even the FBI can show up at the front gate of Disney and expect to meet with the number one and number two guys running Disney. Our initial call went to the head of security, who was a retired FBI agent. This person put us in touch with the general counsel for Disney. After a few telephone calls between Eason and an internal

---

[36] Fictional name

131

attorney for Disney and an external attorney for Disney, we finally scheduled a date and time to meet with Bob Iger and Jay Rasulo.

Our scheduled interviews at Disney were becoming quite comical around the office. You would have thought we were going to Disneyland instead of Disney Corporate Headquarters. I think some of our coworkers thought we might see Mickey Mouse or some recognizable actor or actress.

This would be a one-day trip. We left early in the morning on our three-hour flight to be at Disney Studios by 10:00 am. We did our best to look like the government, dark suits, white shirts, and conservative ties. Eason had his two thick binders full of trial exhibits which were contained in an auditor's briefcase. After arriving at Los Angeles International Airport (LAX), we rented our car and proceeded to Burbank. We arrived at the security gate on time and were directed to a visitor's parking space reserved for us. The first couple of things we immediately noticed about the Disney campus was everyone was dressed casually, and everyone had a smile on their face. I thought to myself, *what a great place to work!*

We were greeted by the in-house attorney and outside counsel, who escorted us to a conference room where we met another attorney. After some initial social necessities, we were cordially escorted to a smaller room outside Mr. Rasulo's office where we met and interviewed the executive assistants of Mr. Rasulo and Mr. Iger. We reviewed authentic documents of Disney and the executive assistants pointed out the inconsistencies with the Disney documents Lucas Jr. had created. One big inaccuracy was on a couple of letters Lucas Jr. had created—he had put the wrong zip code on the Disney address! The executive assistants also showed us authentic signatures of Mr. Iger and Mr. Rasulo. Both ladies made great witnesses at trial.

After completing our interviews with the executive assistants, we patiently awaited our window of opportunity to interview Mr. Rasulo while admiring all things Disney around the office. However, we immediately had to deal with a small miscommunication. To hear what a typical day might be like for Mr. Rasulo and Mr. Iger was to immediately recognize these two gentlemen were as busy as the President of the United States. Their time was valuable so when we were told by the Disney attorneys that we would be given five minutes with Mr. Rasulo and five minutes with Mr. Iger, we were not too happy. We had just traveled on a three-hour flight that left Dallas at 6:00 am for two five-minute interviews. "Yeah, that wasn't going to happen," Eason whispered to me.

After receiving the word that Mr. Rasulo was ready for us to come into his office, we were hastily shuffled in by the attorneys. Mr. Rasulo was finishing up a telephone call when we entered so Eason and I marveled over some of the paraphernalia in his office, specifically Thor's hammer, which we both wanted to heave around. Mr. Rasulo could not have been more pleasant, and we were both taken by his gracious personality.

Eason started discussing the trial exhibits as they pertained to Mr. Rasulo. Promptly at the five-minute mark, the attorneys attempted to wrap up the interview. At this point, I could see the junk-yard dog in Eason was about to be unleashed. With canines showing and ears pinned, Eason calmly articulated to all parties that we had just traveled three hours for this interview and explained to everyone the importance of completing the interview. Eason firmly explained that if the interview could not be completed on this day, then the subpoenas I was carrying for Mr. Rasulo and Mr. Iger would be served and the interview would be completed back in Plano, Texas. The surprised looks on the Disney attorneys' faces were priceless. I believe both Disney attorneys realized it was to everyone's benefit to complete the interview while we were there. I was relieved the attorneys did not call our bluff since I was not carrying any subpoenas. As Eason was exerting Justice Department privilege, Mr. Rasulo's executive assistant came in and said Mr. Iger was calling. Mr. Rasulo said to his executive assistant, "Tell Bob [Iger], I'm with Chris and I'll be late to the meeting." Since Mr. Rasulo's answers to our questions were so complete and direct, we were done within an hour and there was no need to talk to Mr. Iger. I humorously observed the relief in the eyes of both attorneys. I did re-evaluate my initial perception of the Disney campus, *what a great place to work if you're not an attorney.* As we left our meeting with Mr. Rasulo, I laughed at Eason and said, "Chris, I don't think anyone has ever addressed these Disney folks like you did, especially in their own office."

After departing Mr. Rasulo's office, Eason and I had several hours to kill before heading back to the airport, so we decided to put the trial exhibits back in the rental car and take a self-authorized, self-guided tour of the campus. We were noticeably out of place in our dark suits, but I think several people, including some actors, thought we were financiers or something. We saw the building where Tom Hanks filmed some of the Disney movie "Saving Mr. Banks." We walked backstage while they were filming an episode of the hit TV series, "Blackish." Eason pointed out Larry Fishburne, who was sitting in his actor's chair reviewing the script. When my eyes locked with the eyes of Mr. Fishburne, I gave him the 'silent nod' and he returned it. I thought that was pretty cool. After that, Eason felt so comfortable being on set that he helped himself to a bag of popcorn put out for the cast. We walked through the halls where famous caricatures from well-known movies hung on the walls and we even visited the gift shop. All in all, it was an enjoyable and successful trip.

Chapter Twenty-Three
"One Last Chance"

Trial was scheduled for February 9, 2015, but the pre-trial hearing was scheduled for the third week of January. The pre-trial hearing is a hearing before the trial judge where the prosecutors and defense attorneys resolve legal motions and other issues prior to trial. By this time, Lucas, Jr. had hired three additional attorneys.

Eason and I decided to give Lucas Jr. one last chance to plead guilty. We were ready for trial as far as the direct evidence against Lucas Jr. was concerned. However, to spare the judge and his staff the laborious effort of a week-long trial, to save witnesses time off from work, and to save the government expenses incurred for flying witnesses into town, lodging and other costs, we invited Lucas Jr. and his attorneys back to the United States Attorney's Office (USAO).

Lucas Jr. and his attorneys accepted the invitation. This time Lucas Jr. appeared with two attorneys. This was a win-win situation for the defense. They got the opportunity to see exhibits that would be presented at trial without going through the voluminous documents associated with the case. By this time, the defense attorneys had all the information due to discovery, which is the process of the government turning over all evidence and documented testimony to the defense so they can review everything prior to trial.

The meeting was scheduled for early January 2015. When Lucas Jr. arrived at the USAO, he was carrying an oxygen tank with a nasal cannula that extended from his nose to the oxygen tank. He was exaggerating his breathing process and sort of dragged his right leg as he approached the conference room which caused me to chuckle. Eason thanked him for coming in. Lucas Jr. shouted at Eason, "Talk to my attorneys, don't talk to me." I thought to myself, "Man, this is going to be useless." Lucas Jr.'s defense attorneys informed us that Lucas Jr.'s health was deteriorating from the migraines and the stress of the upcoming trial, and he was medically incapable of standing trial. They also advised us that at the pretrial hearing, they would motion the court to continue the trial on a later date.

Eason and I did not believe Lucas Jr was incapable of standing trial. We believed the oxygen tank was a prop to support his continued lies. We made our presentation. We showed Lucas Jr. the evidence contradicting every lie he had told with respect to DFW Disney and how a jury would easily conclude his guilt. Eason said to Lucas Jr., "Since this is a criminal case, I can't call you to the stand…"

"That's right, I'll plead the fifth", yelled Lucas Jr.

Eason continued, "But I'll get to introduce your side of the story, specifically all the lies you told in the civil deposition videos." We then showed Lucas Jr. the videos. None of this made an impression on him.

Eason told Lucas Jr. and his attorneys that he was looking at 20 years in jail but the government was prepared to offer a 5-year deal if he pled guilty.

He responded, "Is this the part where I'm supposed to be scared?"

Eason told Lucas Jr. he should be scared because he would not handle prison well. Lucas Jr. believed he could con the jury into believing his lies just like he conned hundreds of investors. In fact, Lucas Jr. became so ornery at the meeting that he argued he could punch holes in the government's case. He glared directly in the eyes of Eason and shouted, "Your case is weak. I know what you are going to do. I got your queen!" I sort of laughed because I was thinking *what the hell is this guy talking about?! I got your queen? Did he think this is a game of chess?!*

The meeting ended shortly thereafter. As I was about to escort him out of the office, Lucas Jr. forgot to pick up his oxygen box causing the tubes to snap his head backwards. Despite looking silly after this, he shouted to Eason on his way out, "Good luck with your career case!" Never a good idea to tease the junkyard dog.

In the meantime, we continued the preparation of witnesses for trial and we also had to prepare to fight the motion to continue the trial. In our opinion and with all due respect to the victims, this case had gone on long enough.

Chapter Twenty-Four
"Motion to Continue Denied"

The day before the pre-trial hearing, while on my way to the United States Attorney's Office (USAO), I received a call from Eason. He said, "You're not going to believe this." Eason said he had just received an email from Lucas Jr.'s defense counsel. The email had an attached letter to it. The letter was typed and written by Dr. Harvey Jeffries[37]. In a nutshell, the letter reflected that due to the seriousness of Lucas Jr's. migraine headaches, which had increased due to the stress brought on by his undercover assistance to the government, he could not effectively assist his attorney in the trial. Lucas Jr.'s defense counsel intended to use this letter to delay the trial to a later date.

The comment about Lucas Jr. assisting the government with an undercover operation was comical. He had lied to his doctor to induce him into writing a medically official document. Lucas Jr. had convinced Dr. Jeffries that his stress was brought on from his assistance to the government instead of his trial *by* the government. Moreover, the letter was written using legal jargon phrases. It appeared it was written by an attorney instead of a doctor. This continuance of trial was the same scenario that Lucas Jr. conjured up for the investors with his 'delayed' announcements. He lied to

---

[37] Fictional name

gain more time in an effort that something good would happen. Simply put, he lied to cover previous lies.

Dr. Jeffries needed to be interviewed immediately. We needed to confirm he wrote the letter and whether the letter was accurate in his professional opinion. Since Eason and I had a full day of preparing witnesses for trial, I sought out help from two agents on my squad.

I was extremely lucky throughout my entire career regarding the squads I worked on and the agents I worked with. The agents and the support staff were always competent and willing to assist another when help was needed. I have seen or heard of agents and support personnel who were incompetent, lazy, or just unwilling to assist someone else, But these employees are few and far between, especially in the Dallas Division and specifically within the Frisco RA. In 25 years, I have never asked another agent for help where the answer was "no", and this time was no different.

I contacted my good friend, DJ and briefed him on my situation. I requested him to swing by the USAO to pick up a subpoena for Dr. Jefferies to appear at the pre-trial hearing, and that Dr. Jefferies be interviewed. Before our first witness appeared at the USAO for his pre-trial interview, DJ and Skilly stopped by to pick up the subpoena.

By late morning, I received notice from DJ that Dr. Jefferies had been interviewed and served with the subpoena.

At the pre-trial hearing the next morning, Dr. Jefferies testified he typed the letter because Lucas Jr. was under a great deal of stress from helping the FBI. Lucas Jr. had apparently informed Dr. Jefferies that he was wearing a wire to record conversations with his Uncle Chip at the request of the FBI. Dr. Jefferies said that what he found peculiar was that Lucas Jr. specifically requested him to type the following phrase, "Thomas Lucas Jr. is not able to assist his counsel in his own defense." Dr. Jefferies believed this phrase was something Lucas Jr.'s attorney directed him to say. After hearing that Lucas Jr. was not assisting the government, but instead was being charged by the government, Dr. Jefferies agreed Lucas Jr.'s actions were conducted by someone medically able to stand trial.

Upon hearing Dr. Jefferies testimony, the United States District Judge denied the motion to continue the trial. The judge concluded that if Lucas Jr. could devise such a contemptible scheme to mislead him, then Lucas Jr. was capable of assisting in his own defense.

Chapter Twenty-Five
"Pocket Aces"

The phrase "pocket aces" is a Texas Hold'em term. Texas Hold'em is a poker game whereby the players are dealt two cards face down and share in five face-up cards. The initial two cards dealt are face down. This phase is referred to as the "pre-flop." The next three cards are dealt face up. This phase is referred to as the "flop." The next card is dealt face up. This phase is referred to as the "turn." The last card is dealt face up. This phase is referred to as the "river." Betting occurs between the phases. If a player is dealt two aces on the pre-flop, these cards are referred to as "pocket aces." Pocket aces are the most powerful starting hand in Texas Hold'em. Approximately ten days before trial, we were dealt pocket aces.

As the government continued its diligent work in preparing for trial, AUSA Kevin McClendon suggested searching the Internet for key words or phrases contained in some of the fabricated Disney advertisement photos which were generated by Lucas Jr. This started out as a tedious task; however, it paid off big.

We entered the phrase "1215 luxury rooms" which was used in the Disney's Grand Texan Adventure photos that Lucas Jr. had showed the investors. What appeared was the exact resort designs for a hotel in Florida called Palazzo del Lago. In fact, every false photo Lucas Jr. had presented to the investors with regard to the interior and exterior of the Disney Grand Texan Adventure, we were able to locate the exact same photo on the website of the Palazzo del Lago. This included, high rises, shopping facilities, lakes, lobbies, and rooms.

This proved to be a home run at trial. We placed every false Grand Texan photo concocted by Lucas Jr. beside the authentic Palazzo del Lago photo as an exhibit at trial. This visualization of fraud was highly effective when shown to the jury.

I had continued to look for the mystery man that Lucas Jr. took to London in 2007…the person Lucas Jr. had identified as his Disney source… the only person we had been unable to identify or locate for an interview. We did not need this person for trial, but it would have been the final nail in the coffin to take any reasonable doubt from the jury's minds. From a personal perspective, the inability to locate the mystery man over the past year began to gnaw at me.

From an analysis of Lucas Jr.'s bank statements, I had identified Northwest Airlines as the carrier Lucas Jr used to fly to London and Continental Airlines as the carrier Lucas Jr. used to fly back to the United States. I had attempted to locate this person through the airlines. However, I was informed by the airlines that they did not keep records past five years. Had this case been a terrorism case, I would have pressed the issue with the airlines because I know they keep the passenger records longer than five years as a national security matter. My guess is they just did not want to look.

I had contacted a friend at the TransAmerican Flight Organization (TFO). The TFO provides ticket transaction settlement services between the airlines and travel agencies. Several years ago, I worked a case where a local travel agency was burglarized. Over 2,000 blank airline tickets were stolen by a man named Vivaan Khan[38] and two minors. The tickets were sold to co-defendants Amani Hali[39]; Faraji Habib[40]; and Hamidi Njowga[41]. These co-defendants illegally printed and sold the tickets to members of the Kenyan community so those members could travel to Africa for half the price of legitimate tickets. This case would have been a lot more difficult if I had not had such a good relationship with my contact at TFO. He was able to retrieve airline tickets and passenger names, which was vital to the case.

I hoped my contact at TFO could be as much help with the Lucas Jr. case as he was with the Vivaan Khan case. However, I did not have the same luck. My friend was unable to obtain the information I requested. Our dilemma was not only trying to identify the assigned seat of Lucas Jr., but then trying to identify the persons who sat beside Lucas Jr. on the plane. Our hunch was whoever sat beside Lucas Jr. was the final person Lucas Jr. was using as his fantasy Disney source.

Approximately two weeks before trial, Eason and I reached out to Special Agent Bobby Lynch[42], our contact at the State Department in Washington DC. We had explained what we needed from him and he was happy to assist.

About a week later, at about 8:00 pm, I received a call from Eason on my way home from conducting an interview. Special

---

[38] Fictional name

[39] Fictional name

[40] Fictional name

[41] Fictional name

[42] Fictional name

Agent Lynch had been successful in accomplishing something in one week that I could not do in one year—he had obtained a passenger manifest from the airlines… like I said, they do keep records longer than five years.

Eason said we had the name and an address of a possible person who sat beside Lucas Jr. on the plane. This person was Michael Brown. I had Eason meet me at Brown's residence so I could conduct the interview. It was now approximately 8:30 pm but we were nearing trial and had to dispel Lucas Jr.'s last lie.

Brown was a great kid. He immediately confirmed he knew Lucas Jr. Brown had grown up across the street from Lucas Jr. in Plano, Texas. Brown also confirmed he had traveled to London with Lucas Jr. at Lucas Jr.'s expense. Brown explained he had been in his yard one day when Lucas Jr. stopped by. The two got to talking and Brown mentioned he was going to visit his grandmother in London over spring break. Lucas Jr. kind of invited himself to go along and said he would pay for the whole trip. Brown said he and Lucas Jr. were not really friends because of their age difference. (Lucas Jr. was several years older than Brown.) Also, Brown knew Lucas Jr. to be a liar. However, Brown, being a college kid, was not about to turn down an all-expenses-paid trip to London. They had duly departed over spring break in March 2007.

Lucas Jr. had led Brown into believing he was rich. They had stayed in the fanciest hotels, such as the Malmaison and the May Fair Hotel. They dined at the finest restaurants, such as Cipriani's, and went to the hottest nightclubs, such as Movida. They even drove in style as Lucas Jr. rented a Maybach. A Maybach is a German-made vehicle that sells for approximately half a million dollars. Lucas Jr. would take Brown to high-end clothiers like Louis Vuitton, where Lucas Jr. paid an outrageous $1,200 for a scarf.

Brown thought it was strange that Lucas Jr. displayed so much wealth but still lived at home with his parents.

The most relevant issue for us was that Brown confirmed he did not work for Disney, and that he never had anything to do with Disney. Lucas Jr. also never mentioned Disney to Brown during the London trip. Lucas Jr. never went to any meetings while they were in London and never met anyone else while in London. What this meant was that not only was Brown the guy who traveled to London with Lucas Jr., but Lucas Jr. could not make up another story that he went to London to meet the Disney source.

Brown stated Lucas Jr. had mentioned Frontier Disney prior to the London trip and even showed him the slide presentation. Brown thought the presentation was believable. Lucas Jr. never mentioned that the Disney information came from an insider of Disney. In fact, Lucas Jr. told Brown the information came from the family's real estate company. Brown denied that he had been the Disney source.

Pocket Aces! We were ready for trial.

Chapter Twenty-Six
"Trial"

The trial started on a clear, cold day in February 2015, in Sherman, Texas. Sherman is a small town located a few miles south of the Texas-Oklahoma border. Its population is approximately 40,000 and not much happens in this small town but if it does, everyone knows about it. It has a town square representative of many small Texas towns with the county courthouse in the middle of the square. It is the home of a prestigious Division III college called Austin College and is near the birthplace of former President Dwight D. Eisenhower. The most interesting thing to me about Sherman is the Federal Courthouse. The Federal Courthouse is a historical building built in approximately 1906. It reminded me of the courthouse in the movie "To Kill a Mockingbird" sans the balcony. I never knew why the federal government would put a federal courthouse in such a small community, but they did, and we all got used the two-hour round-trip drive to the courthouse every time we had a hearing. We used to joke that we were reluctant to arrest anyone in a particular week because we did not want to make the drive. Anyway, Sherman, Texas was the location for the trial of Lucas Jr. and because of the media coverage, the town knew 'Disney' would be there.

In federal trials, the case agent sits at the table with the prosecutors to assist in any way necessary, such as retrieving an important document, or reminding the prosecutor to do something or ask a specific question. In addition to having the lead prosecutor, the government usually has a co-counsel to assist with the trial. Co-counsels are like backup quarterbacks in football; they may take a few snaps and keep the stats, but basically, they remain on the sidelines.

AUSA J. Andrew Williams (Andy) was the co-counsel on this case. Andy was a former state judge and one of the senior prosecutors in the United States Attorney's Office. He and I had worked together for over twenty years. He was a good friend and fun to talk to. Andy told stories in the same manner as a person who should be relaxing on the front porch sipping a good glass of scotch and smoking a cigar. He used phrases like "That guy is wiser than a tree full of owls," which meant the person was smart; or "He's poorer than a snake," because a snake does not have pockets to keep cash or a wallet. He is fair, honest and has a good sense of humor. Andy is an Oklahoma Sooner, so he and I always enjoyed the second weekend of October because of the UT-OU Red River Rivalry. The loser of this game usually received some kind of sarcastic email, voicemail or door message on the following Monday to remind the other of who won the game.

That morning, the prosecution team had met in the room designated for the prosecution. There was a buzz in the air. We had worked long hours, during Christmas break, New Year's holiday and weekends. The case was all over the news. The jury was in their waiting room, I was on the phone dealing with a witness issue, our support staff was making last minute preparations, Eason was finalizing his opening statement and Andy was reading the sports page in the newspaper. We then heard a knock at the door. The lead defense attorney entered the room through the slightly cracked door. He asked Eason, "Is the deal for five years still on the table if he pleads to one count?"

"No!". Eason responded. Andy jumped up and before he could explore the possibility, Eason told him to sit down. Eason conveyed to the defense attorney that Lucas Jr. would have to plead guilty to the whole indictment.

When the defense attorney departed, Andy protested and said, "It is like the thief on the cross, it is never too late to get right with the government."

I hung up the phone and said, "What the f**k Andy, the ball is on the 5-yard line and you want to call the game."

Eason chimed in, "Not only is the ball on the 5-yard line but we built the stadium, planted the grass, watered the sod, and chalked the field! We're not going back to the deal we offered several months ago… not happening!"

Lucas Jr. would not have taken the deal anyway because he would have had to go in front of the judge and tell the truth. That just was not going to happen.

After the jury was selected in the morning, opening statements by the prosecutors and defense attorneys began right after lunch. Opening statements is the phase of trial where the government discloses to the jury its case-in-chief; it is what the government intends to prove. The government went first.

Eason stoically stood beside the podium and addressed the jury. He began his statement with, "Once upon a time, Thomas Lucas Jr. created a lie; he sold that lie; and he caused others to sell that lie. However, this story does not end happily ever after," and ended his statement with, "Unlike a typical Disney show, there would not be a happy ending." He laid the foundation that even though this case was not about Disney, references to Disney would be made throughout the trial because Lucas Jr. unjustly used the name of Disney to fraudulently illicit funds from investors. He also conveyed that Disney representatives would testify, which seemed to interest the jury.

The witnesses previously mentioned, and more, testified at trial regarding the elements of the statutes. Mark Emerson, Kendal Kent, professional athletes and investors walked the jury through the misrepresentations made by Lucas Jr. and the amount of their losses. Bankers walked the jury through the interstate wires coming from the victims' accounts and being deposited in the HBLCO bank account.

Bob Pressley, Lucas Jr.'s high-school friend testified to a piece of the puzzle that linked Lucas Jr. to the fraud. If you recall, the two fraudulent letters written in 2005 allegedly between Mr. Rasulo and Excalibur Management Group, were attached to an email. The email was addressed to Lucas Jr. at his email address tlucasjr@hblco.com. In depositions and in the interview with the FBI, Lucas Jr. denied he had ever had this email address. In a follow-up interview with Pressley, Pressley had informed me that he bumped into Lucas Jr. at a local restaurant in Plano, Texas. Lucas Jr. provided Pressley with his business card before they went their separate ways. The business card reflected Lucas Jr. used the email address of tlucasjr@hblco.com. Lucas Jr. could not continue to lie about using this email address unless he took the stand. This was not going to happen. The business card also reflected a satellite phone number for Lucas Jr. Again, Lucas Jr. thought he was some kind of CIA operative.

In violent crime cases, testimony sometimes speaks louder than physical evidence sans a bloody crime scene. However, in white-collar cases, evidence in the form of documents speaks louder than actual testimony. In this case, we had both. However, it is nice to have witnesses who either connect with the jury through their delightful personality or through their passion. I believe the testimony from Mr. Rasulo and Mr. Stone was so overwhelming that I knew the jury would convict Lucas Jr. after each one of them stepped down from the witness stand.

Chapter Twenty-Seven
"Disney Comes to Sherman, Texas"

When the government flies out-of-town witness into town, the government picks up travel expenses such as lodging, airfare and transportation. Since it is the government, witnesses fly coach (not first class), transportation is not top of the line automobiles, and hotels are not fancy. The Witness Coordinator in the United States Attorney's Office will contact the witnesses on the witness list and arrange their travel. It is a tough job because in an effort to save money, the government tries to fly the witness in for only one or two days. A witness slated to testify in the afternoon may be flown in the morning of trial. A witness who is slated to testify in the morning will be flown in the day before trial. Since the closest international airport to Sherman, Texas is Dallas, Ft. Worth International (DFW) Airport, the commute time to Sherman, Texas is approximately two hours. It is easy to see why the Witness Coordinator must maintain constant communication with the prosecutor to ensure the government does not run out of witnesses on any trial day. Running out of witnesses never sits well with the judge.

I knew when the Witness Coordinator contacted Disney to arrange travel for Jay Rasulo and his two executive assistants, she would be in over her head. This would be like calling the White House and trying to get the president to take a commercial flight to

DFW at the government rate for coach seating, and then getting a taxi driver to transport him two hours to Sherman, Texas.

When the call was made, the response went something like this, "No thank you, Mr. Rasulo will be taking Disney's private jet." All the Witness Coordinator had to do was tell the Disney people the day and time Mr. Rasulo needed to be in Sherman, Texas. The Disney pilot made the flight plan to land the plane at a small airport in Sherman, Texas. The travel division at Disney made arrangements to have Mr. Rasulo, the two assistants, and two attorneys picked up at the small airport in black Sports Utility Vehicles that resembled Secret Service vehicles and transported to the hotel. They arrived around 7:00 pm and after freshening up, they came down to the lobby so Eason could tell each of them what to expect the next day. I was a little disappointed when I discovered Disney's private jet did not have Mickey Mouse's photo on it or something that indicated it was a Disney jet.

However, as I mentioned, Sherman is a small town, and everyone knows everyone's business. In talking to the two executive assistants the next morning, we learned that Mr. Rasulo and his companions went to eat dinner the previous night at a Bar-B-Q joint just outside of town. The place closed at 9:00 pm but when the restaurant discovered their clientele was from Disney, they were happy to stay open a little later. We heard the Bar-B-Q staff was delightfully impressed with Mr. Rasulo who had them laughing in stitches. Again, the small town of Sherman, Texas hosting the number two guy in charge of Disney was like having the Disney characters themselves in town. This exciting reception carried over to the trial on the next day.

The two executive assistants testified first. They both did an outstanding job pointing out the inconsistencies between an authentic Disney memo and the false Disney memos that Lucas Jr.

had shown investors. Then, briefly consistent with the drum roll heard for the celebrities walking the red carpet at the Oscars, Eason called Jay Rasulo to the stand.

Mr. Rasulo identified himself to the jury with a pleasurable eloquence that endeared himself to the jury. The jury was quite captivated with this gentleman. His testimony on the stand was not the familiar monotone question-answer session I had seen hundreds of times before. This question-answer session was a delightful conversation that every now and then prompted laughs from the jury. There had been few times in my experience where one witness had captivated a jury so much that they were on the edge of their seats. Mr. Rasulo definitely enthralled this jury with his charm and eloquence.

Mr. Rasulo said the one thing everyone in the courtroom wanted, and in some cases, needed to hear. Disney was not planning to build a theme park in North Texas and has never planned to build a theme park in North Texas. His testimony included common business sense. Why would Disney want to build a theme park in the middle of the country that would take business away from California and Florida; and why would Disney want to build a theme park in a place that reaches 110 degrees in the summer?!

Eason showed Mr. Rasulo the photograph of him standing on stage purportedly in Dallas with the DFW Disney logo above his head. Mr. Rasulo confirmed the photo was false because there was no DFW Disney and the stage he was standing on was not located in Dallas. Mr. Rasulo said the photograph was taken of him in New York City celebrating Disney's 50th anniversary. He recalled the ceremony for several reasons, but one was because Julie Andrews, the great entertainer and the unofficial face of Disney, was there. Eason followed up with, "Yes, Julie Andrews from the Disney movie, The Sound of Music." My eyes about popped out of my head while connecting with the bugged-out eyes of Andy. I loudly whispered to Eason, "That is not a Disney movie!" However, Mr. Rasulo did not miss a beat in correcting Eason that although Ms. Andrews gave a brilliant performance in The Sound of Music, she was better known for her role in Mary Poppins, one of the great Disney features. Everyone in the courtroom had a good laugh about that comment then, and we had a good laugh over dinner that evening.

Mr. Rasulo reviewed the 2005 letters allegedly written between him and Ken Webb, Excalibur Management Group. Mr. Rasulo not only pointed out the poor grammar and the misspelled words, but he added the letters were so poorly written that he questioned how anyone would believe them. In reference to Disney executive, Karl Holtz, whose name was misspelled, Mr. Rasulo questioned why any executive would tell a third party about an employee's promotion before actually telling the employee. He confirmed the letters were false and the signature of his name was a forgery.

One last statement that Mr. Rasulo effortlessly dispelled was the alleged automobile accident involving his family in 2008. In an email from Lucas Jr. to his Uncle Chip and others, Lucas Jr. notified everyone that the final Disney announcement scheduled for November 2008 had been delayed because Mr. Rasulo's wife and young daughter had been in a car accident. Mr. Rasulo told the jury his wife and daughter were never in a car accident and his daughter was fully grown by 2008.

I do not recall the defense attorneys having many questions for Mr. Rasulo. After all, what was there to ask after he stated there were never any plans for Disney to come to North Texas? Any questions would just re-emphasize their client was a liar.

Chapter Twenty-Eight
"Nail in the Coffin"

The final witness to testify prior to me was Nicky Stone. He had been an early investor of the land option contracts. Based on the representations made by Lucas Jr., Uncle Chip, and Mark Emerson about the Disney insider, Mr. Stone invested approximately one million dollars because he believed Disney was going to build a theme park in North Texas. Like all the other investors, Mr. Stone stated he would never have invested his money had it not been for the insider at Disney providing maps, plans, advertisements, announcement dates and all the other information. This was relevant because if Lucas Jr. took the stand, the defense attorneys would have said the investments were made because of the Dallas North Tollway being extended through Celina, Texas. Mr. Stone dispelled this defense before it could begin.

What Mr. Stone provided that none of the other investors provided was passionate testimony. The other investors who testified were calm on the stand which was okay; however, if I had lost hundreds of thousands of dollars, even millions of dollars, to a conman, I would have been infuriated. Some of the investors appeared to feel as if it had not been a big deal. Mr. Stone, however, held nothing back which made him one of the most memorable witnesses I ever saw testify. He delivered a testimony that was simple, honest and intensely direct.

Mr. Stone was one of three investors who believed they were being scammed in 2009. So much so that during an investor presentation break, he took it upon himself to take photos of Lucas Jr.'s slideshow presentation. He took photos of the two bogus letters written in 2005 between Mr. Rasulo and Mr. Webb; he took a photo of the fake presentation announcement by Mr. Rasulo; and he took a photo of the fake preliminary concept plan for Frontier Disney.

Mr. Stone explained to the jury that after he, Darius Garland and another investor had located authentic Internet photos of Mr. Rasulo giving the 50th Disney anniversary presentation in New York and the Wild West World preliminary concept plan, he confronted Lucas Jr. and Uncle Chip. He had looked each of them in their eyes and told them if they were defrauding him and the other investors, he would ensure "their asses would burn." Lucas Jr. had admitted to Mr. Stone that he Photoshopped the photo of Mr. Rasulo giving the presentation on stage during the 50th anniversary of Disney to make it appear that the presentation was a rehearsal for Frontier Disney. Lucas Jr. admitted he had done this to get investors off his back with regard to the delayed announcements. A short time after this revelation, Mr. Stone reported the fraud to the SEC and the FBI in Dallas.

When Mr. Stone was cross-examined by the defense, he was asked, "Wasn't it true that Lucas Jr. told you this was an investment in the North Dallas Tollway?"

Without hesitation, Mr. Stone pointed his finger at Lucas Jr. and furiously said, "That's a lie!" He continued to point out the ridiculous theory that if his investment was for the North Dallas Tollway, which was years from being completed, then why had there been a need to ante up more money to extend option contracts for future announcements for DFW Disney? He also pointed out that if his investment had had anything to do with the Dallas North Tollway, then why were so many photos of Disney plans, parks, rides, hotels, golf courses and airports shown to the investors instead of construction plans for the toll road? Mr. Stone's testimony was the nail in the coffin. In fact, Mr. Stone's answers to the questions by the defense attorney were so emotionally honest, the defense attorneys did not keep him on the stand too long.

Finally, I testified as a summary witness and illustrated how Lucas Jr. spent the money he made from his scam. Eason did an outstanding job with my direct examination. He had me summarize the entire case and walk the jury through the web of lies and fake photographs. Unlike our previous trial in the mortgage fraud case, I was quite happy with Eason's line of questioning this time. Using a pie chart, the jury was shown how Lucas Jr. spent some of the money:

Amount (rounded)	Category
$ 100,000	Family member
$ 68,000	Cash withdrawals
$ 45,000	Foreign travel (Lucas Jr. only traveled to London, once)
$ 38,500	Fashion and jewelry
$ 19,700	Hotels
$ 13,500	Savings transfer
$ 51,600	Other miscellaneous
$ 8,500	Cigars and liquor
$ 2,500	Adobe software

So where did the millions go? Some ended up as commissions for the other salesmen of HBLCO. However, the majority ended up in the hands of the landowners; the sellers of the land or the sellers of the land option contracts. Interviews with landowners revealed they had heard the Disney rumors for over 20 years. The landowners laughed at the notion. However, the landowners did not know this was the reason HBLCO was purchasing the land. This was not a crime of greed. It was a crime committed to achieve something worth more than money to Lucas Jr... social acceptance and personal value.

The cross-examinations conducted by Lucas Jr.'s three defense attorneys were noble efforts; however, it's hard to dispute facts when the facts are memorialized in documents. In short, the defense attorneys did not have a whole lot of places to go with their arguments.

The defense called only one witness on behalf of Lucas Jr. It was his father; Thomas Lucas Sr. Lucas Sr. spoke about his son like I expected any father to do. However, on cross examination by the prosecution, Lucas Sr. had to tell the truth or get charged with perjury. Andy did an outstanding job in getting Lucas Sr. to recall a meeting with Mr. Stone and Mr. Garland.

Andy: "LaDarius Garland was on the phone during the meeting with Mr. Stone. At that meeting you were made aware of the fact that this picture (Rasulo photo) that had been shown to investors was false, correct?

Lucas Sr.: "I was told it was false."

Andy: "You were told it was false. Okay. And the same thing about that concept plan from Law Kingdon architecture firm. You were made aware of that?"

Lucas Sr.:   "I was told the picture was false, not the Law Kingdon."

Andy: "Okay. Now those are pretty serious allegations, aren't they?"

Lucas Sr.:   "Yes."

Andy: "I mean if that—if that had been done, that's something you would be very concerned about. Right?"

Lucas Sr.:   "I was concerned."

Andy: "And if you were an investor that had a million dollars, two million dollars on the line with this, you would be very, very concerned, wouldn't you?"

Lucas Sr.:   "Well I didn't have anything invested in 2008 but I know that Chip and Emerson would have been very concerned… I would have been concerned as well."

Andy: "But it's a fact that you didn't contact one single investor after you learned this to tell them that there might be a possibility of some fraud, did you?"

Lucas Sr.:   "Not that I recall… no."

With that last answer, I watched one juror roll her eyes and another shake his head.

There would be no further witness testimony after Lucas Sr. Andy had got Lucas Sr. to admit he knew about the fraud, that the fraud was concerning to him and that he never told a single investor about the fraud. This was something I did not have the opportunity to do during the investigation since Lucas Sr. declined to be interviewed by the FBI.

Chapter Twenty-Nine
"Verdict"

The five-day trial was like the classic Disney movies, a few unexpected twists and turns, but never a dull moment. The prosecution team had put on Disney representatives, professional athletes, a news anchor, bankers, victims, an IRS agent (for tax purposes), witnesses to contradict Lucas Jr.'s lies, and me.

On Friday afternoon, closing arguments were made. The United States District Judge provided jury instructions to the jurors and by late afternoon, the jury got the case. However, since it was so late in the day, the Judge dismissed the jury and instructed them that deliberations would start on Monday morning.

On Monday morning, the prosecution team, the defense attorneys, and the jurors reported to the courtroom. After initial remarks, the Judge sent the jurors back to the jury room to deliberate. Within less than one hour, the jury returned a verdict of guilty on all counts. Eason and I commented about being part of the quickest jury decision in the Eastern District of Texas' history. We joked that the jurors barely had time to select a foreman and drink their first cup of coffee.

As I listened to the verdict, I glanced over to the gallery of observers. I saw the faces of Lucas Jr.'s parents. As his mother wept, I was reminded once again that white-collar criminals not only financially ruin their victims, but they emotionally victimize their own families.

The Judge remanded Lucas Jr. to the custody of the US Marshals. This meant Lucas Jr. went directly to jail after the verdict. In most non-violent white-collar cases, the defendant is allowed to stay out of jail until his sentencing. Even after sentencing, the white-collar defendant will not have to report to jail until a future date. However, in this instance, the Judge did not believe it was appropriate to release Lucas Jr.

Although I congratulated Eason and Andy after the jurors left the courtroom, this was not a high-five moment. Eason, Andy, and I were advocates for the United States and its citizens, so we professionally represented our client(s) to the fullest extent of the law. We had spent many late nights conducting interviews, following up on leads and preparing for trial. Of course, we were happy with the outcome, but investigations and prosecutions should never become personal. When a case becomes personal, an investigator or prosecutor may insert themselves into an environment they do not want to be. They may blur the lines between right and wrong to win a case or record a statistical accomplishment. When an investigator or prosecutor does this, then neither righteousness nor justice is served.

Epilogue

On September 1, 2015, Lucas appeared for his sentencing hearing. Lucas's new attorney was Marsha Bennett[43] who had an outstanding reputation for getting sentencings overturned or reduced. However, what neither Bennett nor the government anticipated was a previous phone call from Jordan Pepperman[44]. Pepperman was a person I was remarkably familiar with and who was currently residing in the Fannin County Detention Center awaiting his sentencing date for an oil and gas scam.

Pepperman was a conman who operated a Ponzi scheme in Winter Park, Florida, and who took more than $3.6 million from people in central Florida. Pepperman solicited investors to invest in his oil and gas scheme and lived off the investors' funds. When the investors got concerned about their investment, he used funds from new investors to pay previous investors. Part of Pepperman's lavish lifestyle that was funded by investors included living in a multi-million-dollar mansion, driving luxury vehicles, and wearing expensive clothing.

Three months earlier (June 2015), a Texas businessman named Jim Baird[45] contacted the Frisco RA regarding a potential

---

[43] Fictional name

[44] Fictional name

[45] Fictional name

oil and gas scam. I was assigned the new case and contacted Mr. Baird. Mr. Baird informed me that he was in the process of buying overriding royalty interests in Cheyenne, Wyoming and Greely, Colorado. The royalty interests were being sold by alleged owner, Jordan Pepperman. The sale was supposed to occur within the next couple of days. Mr. Baird stated he accidently discovered Pepperman was involved in the Ponzi scheme in Florida while searching the Internet.

I instructed Mr. Baird to stall the sale of the overriding royalty interests until the FBI could verify some information. Mr. Baird agreed and texted Pepperman to inform him that he (Baird) had plans to go to the lake and could not complete the purchase of the royalty interests within the next few days.

In the meantime, I reviewed the news story regarding Pepperman and contacted the county clerks in Greely, Colorado and Cheyenne, Wyoming where the royalty interests were located. I obtained copies of the bogus Assignments of Overriding Royalty Interests, which accomplished a couple of things. One, they illustrated the forged documents that Pepperman signed and filed; and two, they identified the actual owners of the royalty interests who allegedly transferred ownership to Pepperman.

After interviewing Mr. Baird at his office in McKinney, Texas, I immediately interviewed the three actual owners of the royalty interests. All three of the owners denied selling their royalty interests to Pepperman and denied knowing Pepperman.

The stage was set for a quick "sting" operation. I contacted AUSA Eason to get him on board with the case and to obtain concurrence from the United States Attorney's Office to record the anticipated meeting. I put a quick team together and briefed them on the ops plan. When we were ready to conduct the sting, I had

Mr. Baird respond, via text, to Pepperman to let Pepperman know the date and time to complete the purchase of the overriding royalty interests. The plan was as follows: when Pepperman arrived, the receptionist would escort him to the conference room which the FBI would have wired for audio recording. Baird would have Agent Skillestad accompany him into the conference room under the guise that Skilly was Mr. Baird's legal associate who would ensure the paperwork was in order (finally, Skilly would get to play an attorney). When the new Assignments of Overriding Royalty Interests were signed by both parties and after Baird handed Pepperman the check to purchase the royalty interests, Skilly would use the code phrase "Easy Money" in a sentence. Upon hearing the code phrase, DJ and I, who would be staged in the breakroom located directly across the hall from the conference room, would enter the conference room and effect the arrest of Pepperman.

The operation went directly as planned. As soon as Mr. Baird wrote the $1,000,000 check and handed it to Pepperman, Skilly commented, "Man, that was Easy Money". DJ and I entered the conference room and immediately executed the arrest of Pepperman. Pepperman was so surprised that his legs went weak and he almost collapsed. He confessed to the fraud and he was subsequently placed in the Fannin County Detention Center by the US Marshal's Service, which turned out to be the same detention facility where Lucas Jr. was located.

Pepperman relayed information that while he was playing basketball in the Fannin County Detention Center, Lucas Jr. came up and started playing basketball with him. Pepperman and Lucas Jr. began chatting. Eventually their conversation transpired to the reason each of them were in jail. Lucas Jr. confessed to concocting the Disney story and duping investors out of millions of dollars. Pepperman described Lucas Jr., who, incidentally, was no longer using the oxygen tank. Pepperman said Lucas Jr. bragged about his scheme. This was certainly more than Lucas Jr. ever told the government. I would like to think that Pepperman contacted the FBI because of the respectful way in which he had been treated during his arrest. However, it was more likely he probably contacted the FBI to provide substantial assistance to the FBI which could reduce his jail sentence.

The information was passed on to Lucas Jr.'s defense attorney and to the court. Unsurprisingly, Lucas Jr.'s plea for a reduced sentence was denied. The United States District Judge harshly sentenced Lucas Jr. to seventeen and a half years in prison and ordered him to make restitution to the investors. This was an extremely stiff sentence for a white-collar criminal. I thought the sentence was rather severe but I was neither judge, nor jury. I merely gathered the facts and presented them.

Restitution exceeded $8 million. Why so little compared to the $60 million he swindled? Since the investigation started so late, we had lost numerous counts because the statute of limitations had run on many transactions. Additionally, the United States Attorney's Office chose to charge only the option contract counts, which amounted to less than $20 million. The decision to only include the option contracts was made so the defense could not confuse the jury by telling them that the victims had land to offset their losses. This was a smart move by the USAO. In the end, only the investors included in the indictment were the beneficiaries of the restitution order. The restitution was insignificant since Lucas Jr. did not have assets to repay anyone.

Lucas Jr. appealed his conviction and motioned for a new trial. On February 27, 2017, the United States Court of Appeals, Fifth Circuit, in New Orleans, Louisiana denied his motion.

The case made international news, probably because of the fraudulent misuse of Disney's name. I received a personal phone call from the Director of the FBI congratulating me on the successful prosecution. The prosecutors received the Attorney General's Award for the successful prosecution of Lucas Jr. This is the highest honor the Department of Justice has. The television show, American Greed, reached out to Assistant US Attorney Eason hoping to produce a show about the case with interviews from him and me; however, the FBI denied my participation because the case was still under appeal at the time.

As for the government, this case ended 'happily ever after.'

As for the investors, it was the proverbial 'kissing your sibling' moment. It is a nice outcome but there is little satisfaction. The investors were happy Lucas Jr. went to jail, but they realized they would never receive restitution from him.

As for Lucas Jr., well, "No man is above the law and no man is below it; nor do we ask any man's permission when we ask him to obey it."—Theodore Roosevelt.

In 2019, I received notice from the United States Attorney's Office that Thomas Lucas Jr. died while still in the custody of the Bureau of Prisons.